WHEN THE SEA SPOKE

40 STORIES & POEMS FROM THE TELLING ROOM

THE TELLING ROOM 10 YEARS

THE TELLING ROOM
225 Commercial St., Suite 201
Portland, ME 04101

Cover and interior artwork: "Leviathan" by Matthew Cusick
Used with the artist's permission.
mattcusick.com

Cover design and interior layout by Andrew Griswold

Printed in USA by Walch Printing

WHEN THE SEA SPOKE

» INTRODUCTION

"What makes me happy is the small things: the rivers I've found, the fish I've caught, the people I've met," wrote Colin Shepard a student at Casco Bay High School. The Telling Room first met him to work on his writing eight years ago and we published his story "Wildernesses" in our anthology, *I Carry It Everywhere* (2008). Like all of the stories and poems in this collection, his story is about the beauty, power, and purpose of water. Almis Isse, who we worked with in his alternate education class at Deering High School that year, wrote about water, too, as he remembered New Orleans after Hurricane Katrina: "It's hard to explain what it's like to see the city where you grew up under water, knowing you won't go back for a long time."

This student anthology comes at a time of milestones in Telling Room lore, as we celebrate our tenth anniversary year and go back and notice where we've been. To date, we have published over 2,000 young writers in nearly eighty books from students all across the state of Maine. Every year since 2007 when we published our first thematic anthology, *I Remember Warm Rain*, we've sat down to write on a specific theme with students in their classrooms, in our writing studio on Commercial Street in Portland, and in fields, on the streets, and at sea. They've taken up our challenges to write about many themes over the years: food, neighborhoods, play, wondrous objects, and wildness. This year, they wrote about water.

One of The Telling Room's secret ways to engage our new students in writing is to share the stories and poems of the students who've come before them. It's incredible what happens when student writers get to read models of writing published in a book of literature by their own peers. Flipping through our anthologies and chapbooks to find inspiration for this year's students, our teaching artists saw that many of our past student authors had already written about water. We shared these stories and poems with current students in our workshops and residencies in their schools, and they were inspired to write their own water stories down. The best of these appear here. This book serves as a bridge connecting our stories and poems from the past ten years with the young writers who will read them and write their own with us in our second decade.

Gustave was a massive Nile crocodile who was sixty-five years old and twenty feet long. Vassily Murangira, in his story "Swimming to Safety," from our student anthology *How to Climb Trees* (2010), wrote: "People say that Gustave is a notorious man-eater because he has eaten over 300 people on the shores of Lake Tanganyika in Burundi, and Lake Rusizi in Rwanda. The last time Gustave had been seen was February 2008, and in our lake." This year, three other Burundi writers write beautifully about water. Author Maryse Dushime resurrects Gustave, Milly Mpundu shows us Lake Rusizi today, and Yann Tanguy Irambona brings us from Lake Tanganyika to the YMCA, where his bathing suit smells like medicine and friends are hard to come by.

Kings Floyd, in "Fishermen at the Pier" from *Exit 13* (2012), wrote: "The fish pull hard and the conversation is sometimes nonexistent, but the fishermen never seem to run out of stories. The question posed twice, over two days, was simple; 'What's the weirdest thing you've ever pulled out of the ocean?'" This year, a group of students from Mt. Ararat Middle School in Topsham spent twelve weeks with The Telling Room in similar journalistic mode, connecting to the water close by them—consider their stories about a river market boat, a shower drain, cat urine, and a dog dish, subjects normally tough to care for or even notice but here brought to revelation, abhorrence, and adulation.

"I put my arms up on my surfboard and let the current drag me closer to the rock. When I hear the sound of my board scraping against it, I close my eyes." So wrote Nick Hutchins in "The Rock" from *Beyond the Picket Fence* (2013), a lovely precursor to the many personal essays here where water serves as comfort and threat in equal turn.

Portland High School student Amira Alsammrai, whose poem "Breathing in The Rain" appears opposite Richard Blanco's poem "Burning in the Rain" in our commemorative tenth anniversary book *The Story I Want to Tell* (2014), and previously in *Exit 13*, also knew how to write about water. Her gorgeous poem includes this stanza:

> I remember one night
> The clouds hugged each other
> And the sky rained.
> That night I hated to stay
> Sitting in my room so I went out

To breathe the roses' perfume
And see the raindrops falling on the paper bark
Of trees washed from the hot season.
I could feel thin water flowing between my feet
And purifying me for a new sunrise.

Water has inspired an impressive array of poetry in this collection—it is stilled, churned, drunk, sprinkled, sipped, and splattered. Into it, things soak, freeze, pour, submerge, dive, flow, cascade, plunge, drip, spill, fill, and drown. It appears as a drop, pool, puddle, and as hail, rain, mist, foam, fog, shower, and storm. In Eddie Sylvester's "Rain" from *Illumination* (2013), he personifies the water. "I am the rain/ I bomb villages, cities, and streets/ I can fall in Australia/ I've skydived in South America/ It's too bad I don't have a parachute." Here, Verónica Recalde and Hannah Herrick do the same. And master poet Mary McColley, our second student to appear in three consecutive anthologies (Cameron Jury is the other one), authors "Bass Harbor Light" in this book, but previously penned "O Acadia" in *Beyond the Picket Fence*: "O Acadia! Acadia!/ Your wild, heaving sea/ Broils white with foam and spray—/ And ever may it be."

Grace Roberts, one of the first four students to write their own books in a single calendar year as part of our Young Emerging Authors Fellowship, published ."Uprooted" as an excerpt from her Telling Room novel *Sleeping Through Thunder* (2014) and went on to win the Founders Prize for it. "I take a slow and shaky breath, preparing my lungs for the possible rush of water. A bird flies overhead. As its squawk reverberates through the clouds, I lean back on my heels and wait. I wait for the trees to hush and for the water to settle. The second my breath slices through the silence, I sprint forward and soar over the water." Grace's words about water are a precursor to the lovely fiction and poetry that appear here as excerpts from the working manuscripts being written by this year's YEA fellows: Lizzy Lemieux, Samantha Jones, Wilson Haims, and Cameron Jury. Look for their books later this year.

Overall, this water-infused collection has heart, humor, depth, and drama. It represents the voices of the over 500 students who wrote about water this year through Telling Room programs, as well as echoes the voices of the thousands of students who wrote before them, and hopes to provide ripples from which the young writers who come after them will grab a pen and write with equal grace and fluidity.

— The Telling Room, March 2015

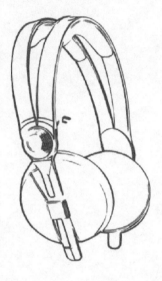

To hear these stories and poems
in the authors' voices, check out:

https://soundcloud.com/tellingroom

» CONTENTS

>> THE PRESUMPSCOT BAPTISM
OF A JEWISH GIRL

AFTER HANEL BA VEJA

Lizzy Lemieux

We stood on the Mars-red railway pass
Toes curling over the edge, fifteen feet above
The river bottom stewing in August—
Rusting leather-seated wheelchairs,
Slatted red-handled, silver-wired shopping carts,
Old-fashioned, newly made, ten-speed racing bikes,
And children's tennis shoes with tongues like dogs.

The Presumpscot boiled like tomato soup,
Frothing with all these things we swam with,
Friendly with them as the fat, female ducks,
And their puddles of sopping bread.

We no longer bragged that we could swim,
But they knew—saw us wet and skinny,
Tan lines buckled around our hips.
We still screamed like children—
We still were children, I think, at twelve.

We hit the water with the sound
Of flesh on flesh, hand to skin.
We fought with the placid river —
Sometimes we won and we drew
The Presumpscot into our mouths,
Above Razor scooters and squelching mud.

In September it cooled and we sat
On the sloping banks with twenty-five cent gum
In our mouths, heads tilted toward the Vs
Of hollering Canada geese,
To which we hollered back
Call and repeat campfire songs.

We liked being heard, liked everything
Until our big sisters came home,
Each of their ankles wrenched, skin puckered, one
Hanging off a boy like a playground tire swing.
Then we listened to the water
Hitting flesh on flesh, hand to skin,
Listened to who we would be
When we resurfaced.

LIZZY LEMIEUX, a sophomore at Gorham High School, wrote the poems "Edelweiss: Portrait of a Great-Grandfather" and "The Presumpscot Baptism of a Jewish Girl" as part of her forthcoming collection of poetry, which will be published as part of The Telling Room's Young Emerging Authors Fellowship and is focused on themes of identity and family history. Her work will appear in Interlochen Arts Academy's journal The Red Wheelbarrow, *the Scholastic Arts & Writing Awards' anthology* Maine Teen Writing of 2015, *and the May 2015 issue of* Maine Magazine. *Next year she will attend Interlochen Arts Academy as the winner of the Virginia B. Ball Creative Writing Scholarship Contest.*

» SAMPSON'S CREEK

Camila Ciembroniewicz

David Berry has a market boat that he sometimes docks in Merrymeeting Bay, the place into which the stream empties. After you go past the town store, though the culvert, and under the railroad bridge, you are out by it in the wide-open river. David uses the dock to tie up his boat some days. I have seen him many times during the summer with his boat alongside it. Before you come around the bend to the dock after the railroad bridge, if it is low tide, you can see the remains of the huge wooden tree trunks that were fitted together for the astoundingly large boats that traveled the river many years ago.

"When I was a little boy, about seven to eight, I caught my first fish there. Center Street was a dirt road, and there used to be a bridge made of some boards across the stream." David Berry has lived by Sampson's Creek for his whole life, in Bowdoinham, a town in Maine that has a population of about 3,000. When he was a little boy he played where my brother and I now explore. When David told me about when cows lived by the stream, and that there was a bridge, it put me in an entirely different picture.

I have explored along the stream from my house to

the Fire House; maybe a mile. I'm not exactly sure how many houses line its steep incline. Sometimes, next to a cliff with the cave underneath on the opposite bank, I find nickel-sized lead coins, but they are much thicker than regular coins. My mother thinks that they are from the bridge, so whenever I'm down by that place, I picture a shadow looming over me, seeing three, half-foot boards over my head and going into my yard. They would lead to right where my picnic table used to be until some vandals pushed it off. Every time I looked up, I hoped that the bridge would be there, but it was not.

Before David told me that the bridge was made of a few boards, I had pictured a large, grand bridge that had buggies and tall sides crossing it, and huge poles supporting it. I kind of like the picture that David gave me better because it is more realistic. It makes me feel more connected to that time period.

"Where did the name Sampson's Creek come from?" Felicity Beede, a woman who lives down the road, wonders. There's a story she tells about Sampson's Creek. Deborah Samson, the oldest of a bunch of kids, had a father who was not a very good man, and he left the family when Deb was twelve. He went to sea, and instead of coming back afterward, he came up to Bowdoinham and had another family. He didn't tell his second wife that he had another wife. Maybe if they had a piece of land where the creek was, they just started calling it Sampson's Creek. The Sampsons who are in Bowdoinham now might be descendants of the first Mr. Samson.

One day when we were out canoeing in the summer, we found some hundred-year-old bricks lying on the riverbank. When I swim in the river in the summer, I can never see the bottom because the water is so murky. After it rains a lot, the water is high and cold and the color of clay. Seth Berry, David's son, told me that sometimes, when it rains too much, people don't treat the sewage that they put in the river, so it is not the best time to go swimming the day after it rains! David says that the pollution in the river doesn't really affect his travel, but something in other rivers is polluting them so that the oysters are dying and he can't sell the oysters from his boat anymore.

The stream is changing. The banks are becoming more eroded because of heavy rainstorms, and the water is getting more clouded because of roadwork. Lately there is more pollution than I have ever seen swirling from the culvert and into the part of my stream that is affected by tides. If I could change one thing, I would get rid of all the pollution. I am afraid that the pollution will affect fish trips upstream and possibly end up with the fish dying because of it.

David travels from the Kennebec River to Bath, to the Sasanoa River, to Robinhood Cove, to the Sheepscot River, around to Boothbay, and finally back to Robinhood. The Kennebec runs into Merrymeeting Bay under the railroad bridge and through the culvert to a small stream that doesn't come up on the Internet, a small stream where David once played, where my brother and I do now, a stream in my backyard with a story about its name... Sampson's Creek.

CAMILA CIEMBRONIEWICZ is twelve years old and lives in Bowdoinham, ME. She goes to Mt. Ararat Middle School. Participating in The Telling Room's residency at her school was the first time she had ever heard of the organization. While Camila was on the third floor of their home working on her nonfiction story, her twin brother Joseph was writing fiction at a Telling Room residency at his school in Harpswell. Although Camila and her brother have their differences, it was quite shocking to hear that they had both been chosen to be published in this book.

» BASS HARBOR LIGHT

Mary McColley

The deep, near-black of royal blue
Hides in the shadows of waves;
Waves that are cold, and salty as tears—
Where dive only fools, or the brave.

Out there—upon the turbulent seas,
White burgeons on falling dark crests.
The wind runs wild along the tall pines,
In a shuddery, salty cold zest.

The rush of water meets weathered stone,
Crashing in riotous spray,
And the pale rain of ocean-swirled foam
Star-spangles the cool air of day.

The westward sun, it glitters and shines,
Lighting slick rocks brilliantly—
And the ivory foam is a cursive script
On the midnight blue of the sea.

MARY MCCOLLEY is a fifteen year old who is utterly in love with language. She penned "Bass Harbor Light" at Acadia National Park, where, true to tradition, she made her family wait ages for her to capture the moment. She plays the flute in marching band, runs track, contemplates grammar, and spends her days at Marshwood High School, where she only occasionally reads under the desk.

» INSIDE THE LIFE I KNEW

Clautel Buba

My story may not be like the stories
the people who live in town
can say:

The Abubaca drinks from the Wubat River
and runs through my village, Balikumbat,
Cameroon.
Abubaca River—
gray soil banks,
monkeys hanging from fruit trees—
mangoes, oranges,
papaya the size of my two hands.
The lines in my hands are like this river.
They bend and spread
like the long, dusty road running along it
from my village to Bamenda,
the bigger town.

When I go to town,
I spend five days outside the life I know.
I see lights, TV, and running water.
But I am from the village,

living with my grandmother,
next to a river
where the water is too dirty to drink.
We boil river water for cleaning and cooking.
Keep a tank full for drinking and washing.
I have big hands from building houses, farming corn,
and growing up at age seven
from hard work.

I.
Dry season —
Christmas is coming, and we are out of school.
It is the season for building houses
from large clay bricks.
Many friends work together for francs.
We work as such young children
from six in the morning to six at night.
We make the bricks by hand.

When you dig a hole
in cracked soil, so hard to dig,
you use a dig axe, a pick axe.
Blisters cover your hands until they are hard.
You go through layers of black, red,
orange, white, and gray,
and then you know you start seeing water.
You have to cut through tree roots with a machete.
Holes can be giant.

Water comes from the river.
It is easy for me to get water anytime
because I live next to the Abubaca.

I don't have to wake up early in the morning
like my friends,
who have to walk a long way
to get it.
Girls carry jugs of water on their heads,
or, if they are strong,
they swing them to their shoulders
or hold twenty liters in each hand
like men.

We pour the water into tubs
bigger than we are
in a metal truck we push to the hole.
We pour the water into a huge barrel
five of us could fit inside—
pour it through a faucet
into the clay in the hole,
mix it in the ground.
We pound the clay,
frame it in wood,
put water on our palms,
smooth it on the bricks,
pull the bricks out of the mold,
spray dry dust on the bricks,
leave them to dry in the sun,
cover them in grasses so they will not crack.
Lay the bricks in rows.

Someone counts them, won't pay for broken ones.
$10,000 francs—not enough for a nice cell phone.
Christmas comes—
we take showers, wear nice clothes,

dance, let off fireworks, stay up all night,
waste a lot of our little money.
When it comes to having fun
we act like little kids,
when it comes to work
we act like grown men.

In the dry season, the danger is the wind.
When the sun comes up it's hot
but at night we all gather around a big fire,
burning cassava, eating, and getting warm.
Hunters build fires in the woods.
Wind can blow and spread fire to the bushes.
Dust storms bring twisters.
If one comes in your door
it can suck the roof off your house.
People get sick from breathing in the dust.

II.
The rainy season comes —
this is a hard time, too.
The time to grow crops —
corn, grannut (peanut), okra, beans, cocoa,
cassava, plantains, potatoes.
We plant corn at the beginning of the rainy season
in a big field that we hoe by hand.
The fields are huge and we are so small.
We farm for survival,
not for fun.

You plant corn as deep as your finger
with your heel —

too deep and it won't grow,
too shallow and the wind knocks it down.
Cover it up and the rain grows it.
There comes a time when
you take the grasses out that grow around it.

Corn is ready at the end of the rainy season.
We break it off when it is still fresh and green
and put it in bags.
We store the corn up under the roof
of our house when it is half-dried.
The heat from grandmother's cooking underneath
dries them all the way.

Rain on the roof,
wavy tin roof,
beats over the corn.
It starts as a single note that you hold your breath on,
And when you take a new breath the song continues on.
When I was little I covered my ears
with my hands and beat them
to hear the sounds change.
As you keep listening it sounds like music.
The water falls off the roof
in straight lines
and dots the brick red
ground.

When it is raining we go outside
to run and play.
Soccer in the rain, sliding in the mud,
dribbling through splashes.

My cousin and I sometimes take a big mixing bowl
from my grandmother's kitchen, fill it with rain,
pour it down over our heads,
and throw it on each other.
When lightning comes — it always comes fast —
and then the thunder, we run,
run inside the house.

Great puddles form in the road.
Cars get stuck.
We push them out for money.
Sometimes people can't pay so they wait
for the puddle to dry.

Danger in the rainy season
is when the Abubaca floods.
It damages the houses we built.
Corn plants get ripped out of the soil,
beans wash up, cassava bends to the ground.

My life by the gray soil banks
of the Abubaca River
was inside the life I knew.
But we were like animals living in the zoo.
Animals who were born there.
The food they eat is the only food they know.
They don't know there's a whole forest out there
where they can eat as much as they want,
do whatever they want to do,
go anyplace they want to go,
and be free.

CLAUTEL BUBA is seventeen, and is a junior at Portland High School. He likes playing sports, especially football and wrestling. He listens to rap music and his favorite rapper is Little Snoop from Louisiana. His story is about how he grew up and where he came from. He really likes being at The Telling Room for the help he gets writing the stories that live in his mind. He wants to give a shout out to his Young Writers & Leaders writing mentor and his grandmother.

» BUCKETS OF WATER IN KIGALI

Rachel Iradukunda

I never really understood how my mother was playing both roles of being a mother and a father until a couple of years ago when I came to Portland, Maine. When I was living with my mom in Kigali, Rwanda, I didn't see any difference between how I was being raised and how my friends who had both parents were being raised. But Stephanie Nyirabazungu was and still is the strongest women I've ever known. That sounds too complimentary and maybe a little bit cheesy, I know; but it's the truth. My mother is on the shorter side with black hair to her neck, and she has a soft voice, even when she is frustrated. If you have someone in your life who is literally willing to lose everything for you, you better take some time and appreciate his or her actions, because, I'm telling you, it doesn't happen often.

I've lived two lives: the first with her in Kigali, where she taught me right from wrong, how to be patient and calm in every horrible, terrible, very bad, no good situation, and how I had to be persistent if I wanted to succeed in life. The second life was two years without her in Kigali, when I had to learn how to behave well as a woman, how to be confident as a woman, how to speak my mind as a woman, and how to accept my different personalities as a woman. She wasn't there to teach me any of that. The world had fallen apart. It was bad. I hated every single moment I had to spend without her.

We lived in a neighborhood called Muhima in Kigali near downtown. Kigali isn't surrounded by water like Portland, nor does it have a lake in the middle of the town. It's just many hills and a few paved streets. It was hot all the time in Kigali. When it rained, everyone thought that the weather was horrible. I never liked to go outside in the rain. I hated it then, though now I like the rain, because rain is calm and nice and so much better than snow. Here everyone walks in the rain.

There were two big stairs outside our house that led to a metal gate that opened into our courtyard. We had a water fountain in the courtyard with a red spigot. My mother used to put a lock on the spigot when the water bill was too high. Water was everything at our house. It was how we cooked and how we bathed and cleaned the clothes. When the water came out of the spigot, we couldn't drink it until we boiled it. I think that was pretty common throughout Kigali, since we all got water from the same citywide water cooperation.

When we ran out of water, we got very busy in the house fetching it from the neighborhood spigot at the water co-op, which was also red and had a long rubber hose attached to it that could reach even the people furthest away in line who had their big, yellow plastic buckets. The whole neighborhood would go fetch it. Some people liked to fetch because it got them out of the house and they made new friends. This public spigot was a half-mile walk from the house, and it sat in an open yard where you paid money for the amount of water you wanted. I never liked to fetch, because I didn't like the crowds. But my mother made me. She was strict.

Laundry in Kigali is done by hand. You need a lot of water to clean the clothes: two full rounds of it—one to clean and one to wash. When we went to high school, my sister and I had to take responsibility for the washing at home. My mother said it was time, because we were already doing it in our boarding school. At home, my sister used to take the bucket to the spigot in the courtyard and bring it to the back courtyard where I waited with the pile of dirty clothes. My sister was the fetcher—back and forth she went—while I was the washer. I rubbed the clothes with a big block of white- and blue-striped soap, and my sister filled many buckets with water so I could rinse them. We knew that the water was precious and that we couldn't waste it. It was really, really good if we had water. And when water didn't come out of the spigot, we had no showers. The priority then became cooking. If you wanted a shower, you had to go fetch. It was on you.

My mother made rules, but she also knew that it was crucial that we knew why she was making the rules. She wanted us to understand why, and she wanted us to give our opinions. So that meant we had family meetings regularly. These meetings happened randomly on their own, but they happened a lot. "Come talk," she would say. And we would all sit down together.

September 18, 2010, was the last day I saw my mom in Kigali. She came to the United States and lived here with my brother for two years, until December 25, 2012, when my sister and I landed at the Portland airport and saw her again. It was an unbelievable and wonderful moment. We hugged and cried tears of happiness.

After I got here to Portland, I went down to the Back
Cove near Hannaford, and I sat and stared at the water.
That was something I had never done before in Kigali. It
made me feel good, and it made me think of my mother's
mother back in Rwanda who is eighty-three. She lives in
a village outside of Kigali. To get there we used to cross a
bridge over the Muhazi River. I can't swim. Not many girls
in Rwanda can. Most of the men swim, but only a few of
the women do; it's not something that their parents teach
them. The river scared me a little when we drove by it. I
liked to look at it, but I knew I couldn't go in it. I sat at the
Back Cove in Portland, and I thought about how I'd lived
two different lives. One here and one there.

I never once heard my mother complain about or
regret why things were the way they were in her life. She
had to be a mother and a father simultaneously, and you
know what's impressive: she always, always hoped for
the best and if disappointments occurred, as they did very
often, she always maintained a positive mental attitude.
And, my friend, I'm telling you right now that if my mom
had lacked self-assurance, and didn't have God in her life,
I probably wouldn't be here writing this story.

*RACHEL IRADUKUNDA is a junior at Casco Bay High School in
Portland, Maine. Her story is about her mother, and also aims to reveal
the power of women in societies and erase all misconceptions about them.
Writing has always been her favorite hobby, and she is grateful for the
opportunity to appear in this book.*

» BACK COVE

Liam Swift

Hands out windows, music blasting, we drive through the city night, fingers cutting through time. The warm summer wind feels like soft cotton candy on my lips. Reaching the point in the road where the grass is damp from the midnight dew, we climb out of the car and are engulfed by the sweet whirring of cars from the widest highway to the darkest alley. As if in slow motion, we run. Cameras in hands, hands in air, mist splashing my face like cool blessings from the orange night sky. We finally reach the edge, where the stone bench sits. Not a child, not an adult—bound by the city lights. The water trickles and licks the sides of the rose granite chunks that make up the peninsula. I breathe in the balmy night air. Scaling down the rocky shore, we step on the sturdy boulders and avoid the loose ones. We reach the last few rocks that dot the end of the peninsula like a small archipelago and sit.

Surrounded by ocean, quietly lapping, swirling, and murmuring secrets carried by the tides, I gaze to the distance while the water plays a trick on my mind, creating an illusion that the glowing city is much closer than it is. As I stare at the vibrant light reflections, I fall into a trance. The mirage dances across the surface and touches my fingertips—washing away the corrosion crusting the batteries of my inner clock. But the lip-lap of the water soon brings me from my reverie, awakening my mind. The majestic columns of light pulse new energy into my soul. I open my eyes to the blaring city reflecting across the water and I rise to meet it.

LIAM SWIFT is a fourteen-year-old eighth grader at King Middle School who lives in Portland, Maine. His passion for urban exploring and photography led him to the spot where he was inspired to write "Back Cove," his first published piece of writing. Liam also enjoys acting, making short films, playing piano, and singing. He emcees a monthly open mic for kids and teens at One Longfellow Square and is a singer/ songwriter who is currently recording an album of original music.

≫ CLEAN LIVING

Isabelle Burke

A pile of dishes fills the sink, leaving an unpleasant aroma of mildew and moldy cheese. The kitchen is horrid. Bugs crawl across the floor, and unopened mail lines the countertops. This is your grandmother's worst nightmare. The dishes in the sink are stacked in every position possible, seeming as though someone was trying to win a prize for an "As Many Dishes as You Can Stack" contest but gave up part way.

Dirty dishes are like a story, a masterpiece. They hold the tiniest details of your everyday life, and are as colorful and fragrant. But one day the story will end. It will be washed away to start another on the same blank page, the same canvas—in the same sink.

After work your bowl is filled with soup made by Susan from church because you lost another paycheck to the bank. The next morning it is full of Frosted Flakes. They helped your kids get up in the morning because of that commercial with the tiger, and you have a job interview today and don't have time to make anything else.

Water washes these stories away. Water is the eraser, taking away the old food and residue. You're glad to see them go. Sometimes they are the remains from a meal you feel could be your last, or from what you thought was going to be a special dinner out, but instead you ended up alone at home eating some limp lettuce with slightly expired ranch dressing.

When water has finished its job, you feel amazing. You feel as clean as the dishes. But it doesn't last long. You open the dishwasher to see a clean, fresh-smelling array of dishes lined up perfectly, but then dirty them up again with another one of your "Girls nights," or worse.

Your landlord comes up to have dinner and a chat. "You got nineteen days," he says. "After that you gotta be out of here. I am sick of you leaving this place such a mess. This place is disgusting! I've never seen it like this — it looks like a dirty pigsty. Look at those dishes! I won't allow it!"

You know now that living the "dream life" you have always wanted isn't such a dream after all, not with all those dishes lying around in dirty water, getting you evicted. You get out of your chair, drain the sink, and go to bed. The water is still gurgling down the pipes as you close your eyes.

Wake up! It is a new day, a fresh start. A day filled with promise and, oh yeah, dishes. But you have put those off long enough, and what is a few dishes? Pop em' in the dishwasher and BAM, you're done for the day! Nope, actually you have so many dishes you get one load in and have to start washing by hand…but you're not going to let that get you down. Once the water is warm and running it is okay to start. Put a little dish soap in and rinse that baby until it shines!

ISABELLE BURKE is a freshman at Gorham High School. Her story "Clean Living" is her first published piece, and she hopes to have more in the future. She spends her free time cheering, dancing, and reading.

≫ GILLS

Katie Thomas

I was snapped out of my daydream by the shock of water being dumped on my head and down my back.

"Ah-ah-ah!" I shrieked. "JASON!" My eight-year-old brother scurried away, giggling madly.

"Ooh, you're in big trouble!" I exclaimed, pulling myself to my feet and bolting after him. I chased him down the sand. Our laughter, mixed the squawks of gulls and the slapping of waves, was music to my ears. Jason and I were city kids who had grown up in Springfield, Illinois. We had never seen the ocean. This vacation was the best thing that had ever happened to us.

Jason looked back at me, and then did a double take. From his mouth tore a scream of absolute terror that brought me skidding to a stop.

Suddenly, I lost my balance and flopped down on the sand. I tried to regain my feet, but slipped again. I glared down at my feet for their mutiny, and screeched in horror myself. My feet were two shiny fins! Where Jason's bucket of water had sprayed my legs lay a sheet of blue-green scales, smooth and shimmering with water droplets.

Trembling, I shook my head, trying to dispel this horrible dream. Salt water sprayed from my wet hair and landed on my shins. Instantly, painlessly, they glued themselves together and layered themselves with more of those dreadful scales.

By now, I was crying with fear. I touched my face with quivering hands. It felt normal, but for all I knew, I might have giant fangs! I dragged my tail and myself over to a nearby tide pool. My face appeared normal, but my hair…my hair was as green as limes!

Suddenly, my mind was flooded with whispers and hisses: "Cursed, cursed… at the touch…ocean water… transform… MERMAID!"

I screamed and clutched my head, willing the sounds to stop. "No! No! I can't… No! I can't be turning into a…a…!" I couldn't bring myself to say it.

I heard feet thudding down the beach toward me.

"Daddy!" I sobbed as he scooped up my fishy body. "What's happening?!"

"Holy— Oh my— What on earth?!" he muttered as he saw my tail, hair, and scales.

All of the sudden, I couldn't breathe. I flopped in his arms, gasping for air. My lungs refused to fill!

"Oh my! You have gills!" Dad yelled, pounding toward the water. He ran into the waves, and lowered me into the water. As it closed over my body, my legs finished plastering together, and the formerly dry skin became covered with scales. I could see my green hair floating across my face, but oh, I could breathe! I expected to splutter and snort when the water entered my nose and mouth, but I could breathe! It felt amazing. I also felt filled with energy, like a baby goat not yet sure what to do with its body.

Tentatively, I flipped over onto my stomach. I waved

my tail up and down like a dolphin and started to push my arms through the water. Then I was swimming, cutting through the white caps like a knife. It was so easy! I had never swum like this before!

Without thinking, I gathered up speed and launched myself out of the ocean and into the air, breaching like a whale. My wet tail caught the light of the sun. The droplets sparkled on the green-blue fins like gems. I had been so worried and frightened by my metamorphosis that I didn't even notice how beautiful my tail was! I landed back in the water and examined myself—my electric-green hair, and my strong, green-blue tail that pumped up and down like a powerful machine. It was kind of cool, but it also felt strange, like my body wasn't meant to be in mermaid form.

Suddenly, I remembered my dad. In my excitement, I had completely forgotten about him. I turned toward the beach and zoomed back toward the sand. As I swam, I felt presences beside me in the water. I had no time to ponder what they might be because I was soon splashing to a stop by Dad's ankles. He looked down at me for a second.

"Geez," he said, and plopped down in the sand.

"What the heck happened to me?" I asked. "I mean, it's fun and pretty neat but…I don't really want to be a mermaid for the rest of my life."

Suddenly, a mermaid with indigo scales rose out of the waves next to me. A merman, looking almost identical except for the fact that he was male, emerged from the water on my other side. Tubes connected their gills to the water so they could breathe.

I edged closer to Dad, and he took a gentle but firm hold on my wrists, as if afraid they might drag me away.

"Katie Thomas," the merman said solemnly, "you've

come at last."

"Uhhhh…" I said, edging even further away, "who are you?" Dad and I asked the question at the same time.

The merman turned to his twin. "Where to begin?" he asked seriously.

The mermaid snorted. "First, drop the whole 'mysterious visitor' thing. It doesn't suit you. Next, let's answer their question and tell them our names, shall we?"

The merman looked like his feelings had been trampled on. "Fine," he said sulkily. "My name is Murk, and my annoying twin sister is Salsae."

Suddenly, his eyes widened. "Another human! Dive, Salsae!"

They disappeared underwater. I turned on my stomach so I could see them, careful to keep my gills under the water. Salsae gave me a little wave, then pulled out a little green bag she had brought. It looked like woven sea grass. She pulled out another tube like the ones she and Murk wore. She passed it to me and quickly showed me how to strap it to my neck. Keeping the other end in the water, I peeked at the shore.

Mom was there, talking wildly to Dad. Jason had been running toward the cottage and screaming that I had turned into a sea monster. Mom had sent him to find Grandma and had run down to the beach as fast as she could.

"Where is she?" she asked, looking around the beach. "What's going on?!"

"Mom," I said, rising out of the water. She whirled around. "I-I turned into a-a mermaid." It felt good to say it, like finally swallowing something that was stuck in my throat.

"Ohhh, Katie!" she cried, running into the surf. She scooped me up into her arms, staggering under the weight of my new scales. It wasn't two seconds before she dropped me. Then she saw the tube hanging out of my neck. She moved to jerk it out, but I stopped her with my hand.

"Stop!" I cried. "That's the only way I can breathe!"

"But…why?" she asked faintly, backing up and sitting down hard on the sand next to Dad. "What happened?"

"Why do you have gills and a tail?" Dad asked.

Murk and Salsae resurfaced. Mom squealed in surprise. I guess they did kind of look creepy, with their purple-y scales and dark blue hair. We calmed her down and introduced the twin merpeople.

Finally, Murk opened his mouth. I hoped he would give me an explanation that would clear up everything. He did—sort of.

"You were cursed as a baby," he said bluntly.

"Wha-a-t?" Mom gasped, her eyes wide. Dad didn't say anything, but I guessed that was more out of shock than stoicism.

Salsae groaned and smacked Murk back underwater. She did her best to explain. "Okay, Mr. and Mrs. Thomas, you worked underwater for a time, right? Getting… what'dya call it… photos… for National Geographic or something?"

"Yes," Dad answered, looking surprised.

"During one of your trips out to sea, you hit a mermaid with your boat. She died of her injuries, despite everything we tried to do for her." Salsae's voice cracked, and I could see she had known the dead mermaid.

Mom's hands flew to her mouth. "Oh! I'm so sorry! We-we never knew!"

Murk had returned and was listening to the story sullenly. Now he broke in, saying, "That's what we tried to tell Draker."

"Draker was an insane merman, an anti-human fanatic," Salsae explained, seeing our confused faces. "Unfortunately, he also possessed what we call the Lamar. It's a gift that very few merpeople have—a magical gift. He had the power to do different things, like telekinesis, cursing, and he had some small healing abilities. But as I said, he was absolutely crazy. Sorcery and insanity... not a great mix!"

"He was convinced that humans were out to get merpeople," Murk interrupted again. "He went completely nuts when he heard about the incident. He cursed you in revenge," he said, looking at me.

"We chased Draker out of the city," Salsae said. "That sort of curse is against the Mer-Law." Then Salsae grimaced like she didn't like what came next in the story.

Murk took over. "We had only just closed the Barnacle Gate behind Draker when a scary jellyfish swam by. It collided with Draker. It...wasn't pretty. Anyway, he can't 'un-curse' you, now because he's dead."

Mom was rubbing her temples. "So, how do we get her back to human form?"

"Yeah," I said. "I really liked being able to swim so well, but I want to be a human again."

Murk sucked in his lips. He didn't like what he had to tell us. "Unfortunately, it's... impossible. We can't—wait, Salsae, the Lamar!"

"What are you?" Then Salsae's face cleared. "Of course! Murk, you're a genius!"

Murk puffed out his chest and assumed a horrible,

wise, sort of look. "Well, you know, with brains like these—" he began, and then let out an "Oof!" as Salsae smacked him again, her admiration gone.

"What do you mean, the Lamar?" I asked impatiently.

"Anybody who comes to be a member of the merpeople through unnatural means instantly comes into possession of the Lamar," Salsae recited. "The only way a creature can be turned into a mermaid is through the Lamar, so whenever a creature is transformed, a bit of the sorcerer's power is transferred into the new mermaid. So..."

"You can turn yourself back into a human!" Murk interrupted, smiling.

"Whoaaa," I said, looking down at myself.

Suddenly, I knew what to do. The knowledge flowed through me like warm, delicious syrup. I dragged myself out of the water, careful to keep my tube in the waves. The others watched me closely. I pointed my right thumb at my tail, and my left index finger at my hair.

"Hay-Kai-Sha!" I cried. The scales dissolved, the tail split into two, and I breathed in sweet oxygen again. I wiggled my toes, rose to my feet, and walked. Then I jogged. Then I ran.

I ran and ran, not caring that I was running in circles around Mom and Dad, not caring that my stride was incredibly un-athletic. I delighted in my muscles stretching and flexing as I ran and ran on the soft sand away from the water.

KATIE THOMAS is twelve years old and lives in Standish. She enjoys reading, writing, and learning. She has a family of eight siblings, all of whom she loves and for whom she is grateful. Katie is really excited to be in this year's anthology with this story.

» CANNONBALL

Garrit Reynolds

The end of my big toe is cold,
for it alone has touched the water.
My feet have slipped apart, one over the other,
captured,
in the cold wet world that will soon engulf me.
This exhilarating coolness has traveled up to my ankle,
beginning the process that my leap has begun.
Slowly,
so slowly,
it creeps upward.
Now it has reached my shoulders.
Tendrils of a splash,
stretch far
above my head,
reaching, trying to pull themselves
up to land.
I close my eyes to protect them
from the water's grasping hands.
I enter the cool water.
I fall deeper
and deeper.
My feet sink,

ankle deep, in the sticky mud below.
I struggle,
trying to break free of the gelatinous substance.
My lungs and throat begin to burn
with the lack of oxygen.
A feeling
of panic
wells up in me —
a worry of never breaking free!
Then
I find purchase.
I give one final push.
I am released.
I break the surface,
water streams down my face,
my hair sticks to my forehead.
The end of my nose is cold,
for a nose is always cold first.

GARRIT REYNOLDS lives in Bowdoin, Maine, is thirteen years old, and goes to Harpswell Coastal Academy. Garrit wrote his piece after an activity with The Telling Room where he had to picture something slowed down, second by second. For Halloween 2014, Garrit forgot it was Halloween so he wore his regular clothes. His costume was a charismatic teen.

» KNOWING WHERE TO LOOK

Patricia Wani

In Deering Oaks, my siblings and I are kings and
queens. We are the leaders, the inventors, the scientists,
the environmentalists, and even the daredevils. When we
weren't meeting new people we were finding new things.
There are lots of things to explore in Deering Oaks; you
just have to know where to look. Deering Oaks offered
us the opportunity to do what we wanted free from the
watchful eyes of a criticizing adult.

One time, while feeding the ducks in the pond, my
brother spotted something unusual in the water. He called
me over to see his discovery. Some might turn and walk the
other way, but we decided we should figure out what this
thing was. We started by examining it. Describing to each
other what we saw. Slowly coming to a conclusion that this
thing in the water was definitely not a duck, but also not
a piece of driftwood. We crept up to the pond, getting as
close as possible to understand what it was without getting
wet. Then it moved. We jumped back. Next thing I knew,
my brother was on the ground laughing nervously. I asked
out loud, "What the heck is that thing?" even though I
knew I wouldn't get an answer. When we realized that the
thing wasn't going to be coming back to the surface, we

walked away laughing to ourselves. Sometimes when we felt we had explored all that we could, we would create a whole new world of our own. We took what we had in front of us and made a game out of it. It didn't matter if that duck had really been there in the water or not.

A day in Deering Oaks Park was always an adventure, like the stories of heroes. They would enter an unfamiliar place in order to get to where they needed to be, whether they knew where they needed to be or not; we would enter the park as if it were an unfamiliar place. They would meet new people who would then play a part in their adventure; we met new people who became a part of our adventure. Deering Oaks was the wardrobe of my childhood that brought me to understand the essence of the City of Portland, but it was also Narnia on its own. Deering Oaks held a lot of beginnings for me, and holds still more for my younger siblings.

PATRICIA WANI, a senior at Casco Bay High School, wrote the personal essay "A Homecoming of Sorts," a small piece of which is excerpted above, in dedication to her family. Although she does write in many genres, she mainly focuses on writing short stories. She loves the arts, including but not limited to dance, music, and acting. Often she can be found babysitting her siblings when not at school, but during her free time she enjoys reading just as much as writing.

» SWAMP SYMPHONY

Madolyn Connolly

Lucy leaps off a moss-draped log, tongue flopping about as she gulps down yet another unfortunate firefly. Triumphantly, she struts back to my side, mouth agape, to confirm her third kill of the night. With a joyous splat and roll in the mud, she returns to her usual post of the mossy log, preparing for the show.

It starts with a subtle crescendo of the fireflies. In unison, they buzz and dive above, getting seemingly closer to the ear with each loudening swoop. Then follows the steady bullfrog bass: Croak, croak, croak, deep-bellied booms of toady percussion. Crack, snap, crack, a family of possums scurry by in a hurry, stepping harmoniously upon twigs and brush. Flip, flop, click, flip, flop, beavers hurl themselves into the swamp's murky waters, pounding their tails against its surface in a steady 4/4 beat. Now for the finale; peeking above the tips of towering pine trees emerges a silky moon, which captures the attention of perching owls who chime in with an applause of hoots.

Lucy barks excitedly and chases another fleeting fly. Curtains of silvery moonlight drape themselves over the swamp's muddy inlets and soft-bellied stumps. She hears my whistle, and we begin our walk back to the cabin, strolling along to the rhythm of yet another summer swamp symphony.

MADOLYN CONNOLLY, a junior at Cape Elizabeth High School, has been attending workshops at The Telling Room since 2012, where she has developed a passion for poetry and descriptive writing. Madolyn's poem "Defying Conformity" was featured in the 2014 anthology, Beyond the Picket Fence. *Her dog Olive inspired this piece. Madolyn loves creative writing, being outdoors, and spending time with her dog.*

» A GLASS OF WATER

Samantha Jones

It wasn't until I was standing alone outside a familiar shop that I came back to reality. It was a small coffee shop, as lonely and quiet as I was. I swallowed, opened the door, and went inside. A little bell rang as the door shut behind me. It was dark in there, cold too; the air conditioning must have been cranked up to full blast. Once my eyes adjusted, I could see that the store was empty except for me—or almost empty. The presence of another human being was indicated by the shadow he cast towards the back of the room. Then the shadow's owner, a small Arab man, stepped forward to greet me.

"Sit down anywhere," he said, breathing heavily. I cleared my throat to say something but just nodded, and then quietly sat down at a small wooden table by a window. The table was low and pressed uncomfortably on my knees when I sat. Like everywhere in Abu Dhabi, the window framed a view of construction, but I was more intrigued than usual by the sight. The strong scent of peppermint and peanut butter alerted me to the shopkeeper's hovering presence.

"What do you like, please?" he asked.

I paused blankly before asking, "Why is it that

everything always appears to be under construction around here, but I never see anybody actually working?" I knew this wasn't the answer to the question he'd asked me, but it was what I was thinking.

"Because it is too hot to work in the day, they work in the night."

"And who is 'they'?"

"Immigrant workers, mostly."

"Why are there so many lovely paved streets that are kept pristine and polished when nobody walks on them?"

"It's very hot around here. And Abu Dhabi is very spread out. Many commuters. Most people drive."

"And why does everybody have so much money?"

The man shrugged. "This is the Middle East."

"Is there a middle class? Because I haven't seen it."

"A very small one, sahib." There was so much to learn about this strange city. I realized I had to bear witness to it all.

"Just a chocolate Danish please, sir. And a glass of water."

I realized I'd never been so thirsty. I was now inside, in a cool and dark shop away from the heat and dryness, away from the sprawling hills of sand and empty, uninhabited wilderness. And yet I was still desperately thirsty. It was as though no matter where I was, I could never escape the desert; as if no matter where I went, I'd always carry some of it inside me.

As the man scuttled off to fill my order, I sighed and pressed my face into my hands. My mind was worn out from thinking so hard, my voice was sore from neglect (I had only just used it for the first time in a few days), my hand hurt from scribbling pages and pages of useless ideas, my legs ached from where the table dug into them, my feet smarted from walking in shoes that were melting and falling apart from the broiling asphalt.

But what hurt the most, what made all the other pains embarrassing by comparison, was the pain in my heart. I had nothing left, absolutely nothing. Nothing but a gouge in my soul that a selfish girl had dug in me as I had looked on and smiled. And what was worse, I'd be going home empty-handed to a boss who would probably fire me. When that happened, there would be nothing left for me in my home, New York, nothing to go back to—and that was the scariest part. I was the biggest idiot in the world for letting this all happen. My thirst grew even bigger, as vast as a drained ocean.

The sound of scurrying and the minty-peanut butter odor prompted me to raise my face from my hands. I smiled unconvincingly at the little man who slid a Danish and a glass of water in front of me.

The Danish looked dry and unappetizing so I didn't touch it. With my first sip, the water soaked my parched tongue and washed the freshness of a clear rushing stream into the back of my mouth, but left my loneliness intact. I finished the glass quickly, paid my bill, and left as quietly as I'd come.

SAMANTHA JONES is a junior at Yarmouth High School, where she is the editor of the school newspaper. She is currently participating in the Young Emerging Authors Fellowship at The Telling Room. This excerpt is from the project she is working on in the program, a novel about a young man finding his feet as a journalist in Abu Dhabi, while pursuing a flirtation with an exotic mysterious woman. In her spare time, Sam loves travelling, learning about foreign cultures, and not studying math.

» RIVERS AND ROCKS

Hannah Herrick

She was my water.
A river drifting gently on.
Her laughter, tinkling and trickling,
like a stream in my ear.
Her strength, carrying me,
Twisting and winding down the river.
Her patience, clear and calm, surrounding me.

I tossed a pebble, and a stick, and then a rock.
She took each one, so small a difference, unnoticeable.
But then it started to build, and block the river's trickle
Tension rising as she took each rock I threw,
Resisting the dam I had built.
Finally, she stopped—blocked and unable to go on,
And she was still water.

Her words, asking why as she crashed against the wall.
Her touch, once a comfort
now pulling and throwing me around.
Her clarity, gone, as she rose and rose, stirring the bottom.
Finally, she broke from the confines of the bank.
Her anger faded as she trickled down a new path,

leaving me.
And it was all my fault.

Stuck in the mud and sticks I watched her,
Flowing on and on,
Away from me.
In my attempt to keep her, I had halted her,
but she was strong, and couldn't be stopped.
So she forged ahead,
A renewed and drifting river,
Yet she was no longer mine.

HANNAH HERRICK is a junior at Mt. Ararat High School. This is her first published piece. Her poem relates a human relationship to the characteristics of a river and the complexities that both entail. Hannah enjoys swimming, volleyball, and taking walks on the beach with her dog. Hannah's greatest fear was spiders, which she overcame by holding a wild tarantula.

≫ DOWN DEEP

Simeon Willey

We enter the tiny capsule from the deck of the pitching ship. There is a hollow clang and scrape, the sounds of the sealing hatch. A dull thud and a falling sensation accompany them. All is quiet except for the low hum of the computer and life support systems. Slowly we sink toward the bottom of the ocean. Our mission is to find new life that lives at the crushing depths.

Outside the thick porthole's glass the color gets darker and darker until we switch on the external lights. Strange creatures and wonderful fauna abound here in the otherwise desolate place. I take notes. Others take measurements. We pass some creatures we are already familiar with—the anglerfish, the fangtooth. Slowly we wind our way around the vents that spew the life-giving materials to the creatures here.

Rounding one of the largest vents, we see below in a large depression a most magnificent sight: a beautiful species of jellyfish. Their color is a light blue, almost clear, and they give off a soft glow that penetrates the darkness. Bioluminescent. They are a foot in diameter and the tendrils trailing them measure three feet long. They move along unhurriedly, gently bumping into one another.

Not wanting to disturb these majestic animals, we move closer, carefully. They draw us in, one after another, until we have all pressed our noses against the glass, and scarcely breathe, so as not to fog it up and disturb the view. No one speaks, and if someone could see us from the outside, I feel sure we would be reflected in their glow.

We have to get one as a sample. Drawing even closer the sub sucks one up into a storage tank onboard the ship. As the vessel turns around to reverse course home, toward the surface of the water, suddenly a huge blast out of one of the vents sends us careening madly sideways. We sink instead into a deeper trench nearby, not knowing which way is up or down.

Numerous red lights wink on the control panel and an alarm rings throughout the hull. The lights outside explode in brilliant flashes one by one as the water pressure crushes them, throwing us into darkness. It is black except for the red emergency lights. Then the master alarm goes off and we see the portholes begin to crack. The aft compartment's pressure hull has collapsed and water floods into the hold, even as the release of pressure from the craft drags us deeper into the dark depths of the trench. Only our tail thruster works and steering is no longer possible. Half of the batteries are badly damaged leaving us with little power. The hull begins to creak ominously.

We have no idea where we are going and can only watch as the needle of our depth meter winds slowly around, glowing red under emergency pulses. We know we are pointing upward because the aft compartment is flooded, and we can try to make it to the surface before our life support systems and batteries die. But something in each of us has been altered. It is awhile before I realize that we still haven't spoken. Not to each other, not to ourselves. We sit in the darkness not knowing what to do, and we are strangely unperturbed.

Abruptly the top of the sub was pushed in as if a giant had punched it. We all move to our stations, sure it is time to go. It is now or never. We turn on the rear thruster and shoot toward what we hope is the surface. The sonar warns us if we are getting too close to the jagged rock walls. If we were to touch them at this speed the rock would easily rip our hull in half.

We watch the depth meter's needle moving toward zero, and finally reach the surface. The research marine vessel approaches, picks up our sub, and puts it on the deck. We climb out and tell the crew our harrowing tale. It is the first time we have spoken and our voices are wobbly and make us remember the new species of jellyfish. We retrieve the tank, but something keeps us there together, looking at it another moment in silence. Then they haul it and us off of our sub, eager to show it to the scientists onboard the research boat. We do not feel the adrenaline of fear; instead, we seem to be glowing.

SIMEON WILLEY lives in Gorham, Maine, and is a freshman at Gorham High School. He wrote a story about underwater researchers and their brush with death. Simeon is a Life Scout with a Boy Scout troop in Windham. He plays classical guitar and is on the Falmouth-Gorham robotics team.

» SWIMMING LESSONS IN THE DESERT

Madeleine Scholz-Lague

The hot summer sun
is shaded over by the maternity pool,
but not the grownup pool.

The grownup pool has a plastic waterfall in the corner,
and is too deep for my feet to touch.

The concrete
that surrounds the grownup pool
pokes into my little thighs.

The grownup pool is where I am learning
to swim.

Instructors take turns
putting their arms around my waist
to let me use them for support.

Without warning one pulls me under!
Water fills my nostrils
and panic is in my chest.

Under, water is blue
and chlorine stings my eyes.
Time underwater goes slower.

At the end of practice
I grab a Dum-Dum.
The mystery candy mixes with the sour flavor of fear
and tastes like paint.

MADELEINE SCHOLZ-LAGUE is an eighteen-year-old writer from Gorham, Maine. She wrote this autobiographical poem about the horrors of first learning to swim in a pool in the Arizona desert. She has an obsession with burritos and plans to live somewhere that never requires a winter coat.

≫ A RIPPLE ALL AROUND US

Wilson Haims

As we stand on the finely ground sand of the beach, a speck on the horizon comes closer. When I figure out what I am looking at, I feel like I have cracked a code. An aged wooden hull is attached to a blue mast that flies in the sky proudly, like a country's flag. On the shore, Nate jumps in the water with the excitement of the unexpected, splashing us all. The siblings giggle together.

"Where are we going?" Nate yells into the wind.

"I have no idea! Are we really getting on that boat and leaving the lagoon?" I ask him nervously. "I'm not sure I want to be in the middle of the Pacific in a tiny boat."

"Another adventure arises!" he cries. I say nothing and close my eyes.

As my eyes are shut, I think. We are actually in the Marshall Islands…meeting Nate's biological family…and we are going out into the open ocean. I take a deep breath and open my eyes to confirm that everything that just flew through my mind is true. And it is.

The boat, which resembles one you would see on a tiny lake, glides right into the sand bank next to Lucia, who has been waiting for it. She greets the short, stubby man, who looks to be around thirty, at the helm. I hurry over and shake his hand as well.

"Where are we going?" I ask very slowly so that he might understand me.

"To another island," he answers me.

"You can speak English?" I say with surprise.

"No." He leans back and adjusts the sails with a sigh. I look at him curiously.

"What?" I ask him, squinting my eyes in the sunlight. He begins to sit up but falls right back over again with laughter.

"Of course I can. I am sitting here speaking right to you!" I look away and blush at my stupidity.

"Well, I don't meet many people around here who can speak English, so it comes as a surprise."

"Fair enough." He smiles.

Nate and his siblings are already on the boat, and Nate's biological mother stands in the water, looking at me, his adoptive mother, approvingly. She is proud of the work she has done by arranging for a captain who can speak English.

She leaps onto the boat gracefully as I struggle to pull myself up. She climbs over the man who is sailing the boat and reaches for my wrists and tugs me up and over the side. For a woman of her size and width, she is much stronger than she looks. I gasp and fall over onto my side even though I did nothing to get myself into the boat.

As we tear away from the shore, I watch men smoking tobacco. They are propped up on their elbows waving to us, bidding us farewell. I cannot help but smile. They look so simple, so humored by a small boat pulling away.

On the mast of the boat there is an engraving that reads, in a fancy font, "Outrigger Canoe." The kids stand on the bow of the boat like mermaids on the front of a huge ship. They lean as far as they dare and pretend to push each other off into the water.

I almost say something until I remember Nate's words: "Another adventure arises." He is cautious enough that I am fairly sure I have nothing to worry about. I close my eyes again. I can still see the light with my eyes shut. It looks red, beaming through my skin.

We are cutting through the thin water quickly, like shearing paper with a good pair of scissors. I enjoy the speed and the sense of freedom. I haven't noticed until now that being on an island can really take its toll on you. The confinement is subtle, but in a way it shackles you and you don't even recognize it until you move away from it. Then again there is a surge of coldness and the feeling that you have abandoned the only place that ever truly cared about you.

As I look at the water, I see glimpses of color beneath the surface. I know they are fish, the kinds that live freely here but that you find in a fish tank everywhere else. I don't speak for the rest of the ride in the lagoon. I find it refreshing. There is nothing that disturbs me while we are on the boat. Everyone else is looking around quietly, too. I read their thoughts.

The sinking world around us says enough. There is a word for what the people here are feeling. We do not have that word in our language. In places their land is only inches above sea level. In ten years it will all be under water.

We finally break free from the lagoon and into the open ocean. There is a ripple all around us. Not of water but just a feeling. Nate's family has never been off the island or out of the lagoon. The only one who has is the captain. Even he, I can tell, sees it differently when he is with us, who have never seen such a thing. I stand up and crawl toward him.

"Excuse me?" I yell over the breeze made partially from the motion of the boat, and partially from the natural wind.

"What can I do for you?" he replies, staring at his work.

"Who exactly are you?" I ask, cringing, hoping my question doesn't come across as rude.

But all he does is chuckle. "I am your boy's cousin… Well, second cousin."

"Really?" He is wearing a white baseball cap with the words "Red Sox" written in fancy red letters. Does he know what the Red Sox are? He shifts the hat around and lifts it up to scratch his head.

"Yes," he says. "Really."

"Please excuse my asking, but how did you learn to speak English?"

He shrugs. "It is a given. Now that the water is coming in closer, we need to know how to speak another language. My papa was smart and taught us young, expecting that this would happen." I nod and move back to my seat, suspecting that I have asked too much.

I can now see a small green island appearing in the distance. When I say a small island, I mean a tiny dollop of land. I can feel the energy rising and excitement building as we sail closer.

The water is all around us, now seeming vaster than ever, but I focus on the land. I feel a surge of safety. The water is unpredictable, anything could happen. It is the body of what is so unknown to us and flows with one fluid motion. I don't feel safe on it.

But looking across the boat, I see my son looking at the water. He is very much of the water—graceful, solid, and calm. Everyone from these islands is. They grow up treating the ocean like a family member, and somehow he can feel it that way, too.

WILSON HAIMS lives in Portland, Maine, where she attends Merriconeag Waldorf School. Her love for writing first blossomed at The Telling Room in fifth grade. Now in eighth grade, she continues to enjoy her time there in the Young Emerging Authors Fellowship program, where she is working on a novel about a mother and the son she adopted from the Marshall Islands. When they visit the islands to reconnect with his birth family, both mother and son find themselves at a crossroads. Wilson enjoys being with her family and dog and loves reading, writing, and being out in nature.

>> WHEN THE SEA SPOKE

Natalie Murphy

"How did the sea speak to me? I thought you might be asking sometime soon. Well, I remember it like it was yesterday. It happened the summer after I graduated from high school, on a hot August day. I had been lying on the floor all afternoon, too sweaty and tired to get up. It's been a failure, I remember admitting to myself.

"I had moved in with my grandparents—they'd be your great-great-grandparents, I guess—here on Vinalhaven, in the hopes of earning some money and meeting new people. I hadn't been successful in either department. My mother had urged me to stay in Idaho— her parting words were about our family. She warned, "Your father's family has a history with the sea," as she watched me climb onto the bus. Of course, I knew what she meant; my dad died in these waters when I was young. But since my mother had moved inland with me and we had never returned, I was curious, and went anyway.

"But Idaho was far from my mind that afternoon, you see. I was lonely and confused and passionless, and painfully aware of the party that night at Grinden's Cove. I wasn't going; I had no friends to go with. Feeling like I was being suffocated by my future and the stale attic air,

I ran down the stairs and started my truck. I drove east across the island, and in the sun's final rays, slowed onto the dirt road to Calderwood Point. I parked, and walked down onto barnacled bedrock.

"It was the time of day when the pale sky has just begun purpling into darkness above the horizon. Standing with my back to the northern winds on the island's easternmost peninsula, for a moment I felt the weight of the entire continent behind me. I realized that I could distinctly hear each voice hissing and spitting in the vast choir underfoot. They were crabs, scuttling beneath the seaweed in the briny darkness, making it sound as if the beach itself was alive. I listened to their crustacean jaws bubble and click, sounding like a rising boil across the low tide. My focus on the sound drowned out the crash of the waves and like a lightning bolt I realized what my seafaring ancestors before me had understood: the ocean held more than salt and buoys and my grandfather's dinghy... it was alive.

"I ran with bare feet into the waves with the excitement of a child—no bigger than you, was I then. As the water lapped around my knees, I swear I could hear each sea snail across the Atlantic slithering steadily along the ocean floor, each fish drawing oxygen into its lungs with a watery whisper, and every seal in the bay flapping its tail beneath the waves. An aquatic symphony. I urged to find the unknown! The clicking, scuttling, slithering, whispering, living unknown! The sound of the crabs triggered in me recognition of the ocean's vitality, a vitality that I wanted to share. Like many men before me, I felt the primal tug of the sea.

"My Uncle Silas's words from years ago came back

to me in a rush. You remember your old Uncle Silas? He
was a captain on the Bering Sea. Well, we keep in touch
these days—us old people have to—but at that point the
last I had seen of him was at my father's funeral. I could
remember myself, standing pale and young beside my
father's casket as Uncle Silas placed a hand on my shoulder.

"'The sea giveth, and the sea taketh away,' he
murmured before stooping down to look into my eyes.
'Salt water ran in your father's veins. The sea spoke to your
father and grandfather, the sea speaks to me, and the sea
will speak to you. Come find me when it does.' Mystified,
I had nodded in agreement. I never imagined I would
someday say these same words to you.

"But the next morning as I hauled my packed bags
down from the attic, I knew the sea had spoken to me, and
I knew I must go to Uncle Silas. Until then the surging
Atlantic had only taken from me, taken the life of my
father. It was time to see what it could give."

I inhale deeply from my pipe and look down
at my granddaughter, her tanned face screwed with
concentration. Like a sailor's as he faces the ocean swells.

"I'm glad you came to me," I tell her. "Now tell me,
how did the sea speak to you?"

She begins, shakily. "It all started as I was walking
home from school this morning..."

*NATALIE MURPHY is a resident of Islesboro, Maine, where she is a
senior in high school. Her piece "When the Sea Spoke" is a result of her
coastal upbringing. Seeing the stress that living on an island could cause
in her community, she wanted to express the mystical power of the sea in
a positive light. She is enrolled in college in upstate New York next year,
and will miss the salty sea breezes.*

» FISH HOOKS

Emily Denbow

You live here
You swim in oxygen
Stand brittle beside a tree
And humble beside the ocean

Upon disrupting the sky-bleached
Surface where oxygen
Disperses and wintry water
Carries salt to your eyes and ears

This world swallows you
Entirely in shreds of gray and green
The creatures processing
Breath through their atmosphere

The sun only does so much here
And visitor, you are only graceful
Where you come from,
We are worlds apart

I don't breathe right where
You come from; anxious gasps —

Erratic currents understand
The neurosis roving my veins

I have lived here just below
The splintered tides of the ocean
Reaching for the glassy
Brown surface of the lake

Hoping away the mud and all
The foggy looming memories
Escaping made sea glass wounds
Blessings but the ocean

It still held voices
Like shark teeth and
Madness like waves
More violent as it stormed

Love tastes like
Fish hooks and blood
Like the breathlessness
of a dying lunch catch

Washing up on silk sands
Or rocky coasts
Romantic but rugged,
Flesh torn from abrupt arrival

I don't belong here

EMILY DENBOW is finishing her senior year at the REAL School in Falmouth. Although raised in Windham, by her sophomore year she knew she needed a more creative team of people on her side and transferred to REAL. Always a writer, writing continued to support her and break open the way to a career in writing and editing, ultimately leading up to a publishing internship at The Telling Room. She lives tenaciously by Bryce Courtenay's quote, "First with the head, then with the heart," from The Power of One.

>> BUOYANCY

Meagan Thomsen

I touch water every day. Wash my hands in it. Take a shower in it. Drink it. But most of all, I jump into it. I launch myself into a six-lane, twenty-five-yard-long, fourteen-foot-deep hole filled with gallons upon gallons of chlorine-infested water. I am in a pool almost every day, because that is the life of a swimmer.

Swimmers live in the water. Ever since I was seven years old, the pool has been where I have spent multiple hours a week training my body. After I dive into the water, I am beneath the surface. I am so completely drenched that I don't feel it on my skin. I talk with my teammates about this effect, and we ask, "If you are fully submerged underwater, are you really wet?"

Pushing myself to glide through the pool pumps me full of adrenaline. Nerves take control. Poised for the dive into the pool, waiting for the buzzer, is only the beginning. During the race, the buoyancy of the water keeps me afloat stroke by stroke. One arm out of the water switches with the other one. At the end of the race, I have no energy left. I left it all in the pool. I ungracefully hop out onto the deck and walk with Jell-O legs. Water drips from my nose and I wipe my face only to find out that my hand is equally wet.

I grab a towel and dry off and think about the second that I will get back into the chilly water.

The water is full of millions of thoughts that swimmers have left behind. During practices, anything runs through the mind—song lyrics, or what's planned for dinner, or whether the dog got fed. Then, as we race, the intangible grasp of the silent air transmits from the water our mantras—"Go faster," "Push it," "You can do this," "You've been training for months for this very moment!" The water holds everybody's secrets long after the last swimmer has climbed out of the pool and the ripples smooth out.

Water is a liquid that humans just can't live without. Personally, I could not live without pool water. The feeling of slipping into it and jumping up and down in the shallow end because it's too cold will never get old. Once I take that first stroke, the water suddenly becomes the perfect temperature, and I go off and swim into the blue.

MEAGAN THOMSEN is a seventeen-year-old senior at Gorham High School. She has been a competitive swimmer since the age of seven and wrote "Buoyancy" as a way of describing not only the physicality, but also the mentality of swimming. When she is not in the pool, she finds herself helping inexperienced swimmers with her knowledge of the sport.

>> OUT OF THE LITTER BOX

Noah Burck

Dear Cheeks the Cat:

Your habit of urinating on the floor every morning has been detrimental to the three humans who generously room and board you in this house, the house itself, the three other cats, and you. It is unwelcoming to the humans who wake up to your pee on the floor. Your daily pee puddle damages the wood floor, and the other cats have to walk around or through your urine to reach the litter box, and your own health is compromised. You rarely exercise, so along with using the stairs, getting in and out of the litter box is one of the only ways you are otherwise able to strengthen your weakening muscles.

This urination started when you first arrived at our house. It only took a few days to discover that you were the culprit. Despite your shameless disregard for the use of a litter box, we kept you. This was in fear that other families would not tolerate it and have you murdered. However, my preference of you peeing on the floor to you being killed does not mean that you are welcome to pee on the floor as you please. When I get up and walk downstairs to use the computer and find a puddle of your pee on the floor, it is not a welcoming sight. If there is a hell, it is walking into the same room to find your pee on the floor for eternity.

Now, we give you your food, treats, and pretty much everything that you need to survive, including plenty of water—maybe too much. If the fact that you are being terrible to the people who keep you alive isn't a reason enough to stop peeing, why don't I just tell you how it feels?

You wake up in bed. You pull on some sweatpants and walk across the room, dodging the dirty clothes strewn across the floor. You feel cold, and decide to put on a shirt. You walk back across the room, again dodging the dirty clothes strewn on the floor. You pull out the drawer in your dresser and search for a shirt that you wouldn't usually wear in public. You dig under the three Neutral Milk Hotel shirts, and pick out a shirt that depicts garlic scapes. You walk back across the room. You open the door, walk over to the stairs, and begin to descend. You think about how terrible it is that your cat pees on the floor. You reach the bottom of the stairs and turn to the right to enter the computer room. In an instant, the smell hits you.

The pee attacks you with its wall of stench. Despite this terrible odor, you continue. You walk into the computer room and sit in the chair. You turn on the computer. The odor tears through your smell receptors, leaving a temporary but lingering unpleasantness in your nose. The puddle, sitting in the middle of the room, slowly stretches toward the bookshelf. The yellow pool of liquid emits its chemical weapon slowly, as if it's trying to make its murder of your nose unnoticed. But you are entirely aware of this wall, and it is killing your nose. Your nose is dying. It is in pain. As many smart people have said, the world will end with a whimper, not a bang. This is true as well with your nose. You can no longer smell.

This is what I experience every weekend. I understand that you are a geriatric, and don't like having to climb over and into the box, but—

I take back what I said earlier.

Stop doing it. Please.

NOAH BURCK, who is in the seventh grade at Mt. Ararat Middle School, is the author of other classics such as "Elmer Blossoms' Ballpoint Pens" and "The Cat Who Wants to Eat Mickey Mouse," and a few songs, such as "The Unicorn Song" and "The Vampire Song." When he is not plotting world domination, Noah enjoys playing classic video games, the ukulele, and Neutral Milk Hotel.

» INTREPID

Natalie Burch

I have been sailing for as long as I can remember. By the age of eight, I was comfortable making day trips with my trusty crew: my six-year-old sister and five-year-old brother. My siblings and I had a sail kit for our dinghy, which we could attach in about ten minutes with shackles and knots. We could take out our larger sailboat, but it required some serious strength to raise the sails. The ten-foot dinghy had adequate space for the three of us. Each day we packed some rations, a gallon of water and a box of goldfish, and headed out for somewhere to explore. We also brought along a plastic container that had once held grocery store cookies to bail water out of our boat in case we tipped too far. Most days we sailed around in our harbor, which was never very windy, and our small vessel could usually handle it. Our parents worked on the other side of the island, and we were free to go whatever we wanted as long as we wore life jackets.

One particular day, the wind was gusting from the south, and we were excited because we knew that the strong wind would get us quickly out of the harbor. We sailed upwind to the point of the island where the New Meadows River widened into a larger bay, speckled with sunlight and lobster buoys. Rounding the point, we turned downwind. Warm gusts filled our single striped sail, and the minimal weight of the boat allowed us to skim the waves, picking up speed.

Sailing downwind is much quicker than sailing upwind, we had learned, because you can take a direct route rather than tacking back and forth. We decided to head back upwind after a while, still allowing ourselves plenty of time to reach home. Turning back into the wind, the voyage became choppy as we careened over the swells. I had capsized the dinghy before, once just in February, so I was careful not to pull the sail too tight or turn sideways to the wind. I held the main sheet in my hand rather than cleating it, in case I had to release it quickly to prevent us from flipping. The wet rope chafed at my flesh but I ignored it, as my priority was to keep the boat upright.

The gust that hit us struck with so much force that the plastic connector we had shackled the sail to tore out of the boat, and the sail whipped around, wrenching the boom from the mast. The three of us immediately ducked to avoid being struck in the head with the boom, which flapped freely and heavily at the bottom of the sail. When the gust let up, my crew went to work. Isabel grabbed the rope that controlled the sail and held it down to where it had torn from, and Tristan held the boom to the mast, stretching the sail straight so it was usable again. I steered toward the nearest shore, which happened to be on the opposite side of the bay that we wanted to be on, because the land there would provide some shelter from the wind.

Somehow we continued tacking into the wind, making headway and avoiding collisions with moored boats. My smaller siblings' strength did not waver. All

three of us had on our life jackets, and that was all the
security we needed. None of us doubted that we would
make it and we made some progress getting home.

We were laughing and joking when we beheld a
familiar sight: the two red sails of Aurora, a cat yawl
belonging to our favorite neighbor Mike. He spotted us
from across the bay, and headed toward us to say hello.
Thanks to Mike, we were home within the hour. We
dismantled the destroyed sail kit, and carried it into the
woods to stash the broken pieces. After hurrying up the
hill to the house, we hung up our life jackets on coat hooks
made of cleats and headed for the dinner table, ready to
feast and share the story of our adventure.

*NATALIE BURCH, a student at Mt. Ararat High School, just wanted
to write a fun story about a time when she went sailing with her brother
and sister. She accomplishes that here. She misses the days when she lived
on Long Island in the New Meadows River, but still makes her home as
an island girl, on Orr's Island, in Harpswell.*

>> A PROMPT FOR WRITERS: FREEING THE FISH

Cameron Jury

The milk jug sat comfortably in my hand, between my fingers. It was no longer filled with white milk, but with stale seawater and a small fish that was soon to be set free. It was high tide and salt water covered the shore. I felt bad for the fish. We had captured him weeks before and he had spent his days living in a lobster tank beneath my deck. He was the only fish in the tank; therefore, he was always alone.

The sun's rays beat strongly on my face as I waded barefoot through the water. My blue sunglasses were tangled in my braids. While everyone at the beach party swam and played cheerfully, I wandered off, down to the far end — the dangerous part. I felt dragged there as if by a magnet. This part of the beach was covered with sharp rocks and strong waves and the unknown. But the unknown never bothered me.

I felt the barnacles beneath my feet threatening to cut through my skin. I stepped carefully so I would not fall. One wrong step and I could be sucked into the ocean. It reached my mid-shins, sometimes to my kneecaps. The water around me swirled in dangerous pools. The sea was murky, as if it were hiding something magical from hopeful, watching eyes, and keeping a secret beneath its ever-moving waters.

My toes were so cold that they had no feeling whatsoever, and my body seemed to be sending all its heat to my head. My thoughts followed my temperature, moving swiftly down and inward as if carried on a breeze. I listened to my heart.

As I watched the fish maneuver through the churning current, I stood and wondered about how the world works. How we can take away a creature's life without feeling sorrow, or we can let it live and continue on its path. One last reflecting scale caught my eye before the waves came and took it out to sea.

The Story Behind the Story: A photograph I took inspired me to write this piece. I told the true story of the picture and then added elements and details to make it fictional. While I wrote, I looked at the picture. Through this process, I discovered that I honestly like writing from memory much more—it was hard to stay true to the photograph, and I didn't know how to end the piece.

Story Prompt: Try looking at a photo and writing a fictional story from it. Then explain what's going on in the image or maybe try writing about the backstory behind the picture. See if what you wanted to write about came out as you'd first pictured it in your mind, when looking at the photograph.

CAMERON JURY *is in eighth grade at Scarborough Middle School. She has been working with The Telling Room for four years, and is part of the Young Emerging Authors Fellowship program where she is writing a guidebook filled with prompts (like the one here), poetry, comments, and advice for other young writers. With its publication, she hopes to inspire readers and help all writers conquer writer's block in the future. Her poems have been published by The Telling Room in* Illumination *(2013) and in* Beyond the Picket Fence *(2014).*

≫   WHEN RAIN AND RIVER MEET

Alexandria Collins

When I was in kindergarten we moved to a house on Water Street in Lawrence, Massachusetts. The house was at the very bottom of a hill that elevated much of the city, and the Merrimack River ran behind the houses across the street from us. Whenever it rained my father would have to sweep leaves and trash off the grate so water wouldn't flood the sidewalk.

I remember one storm that struck when I was in fourth grade. After it started raining, my mother came into my room. She told me to pack some clothes and a few books into a bag. "Why?" I asked her. "Just in case," she said. What did she mean? I wondered. Nevertheless, I packed my bag. Then I went to the window. I was scared by what I saw.

Water had enveloped the street. It raced down the hill from both directions, small streams at the tops, but slowly building. It was taking everything in its path: dirt, trash, bugs, leaves, even toys that had been left lying around outside. I watched these things swirl around and around on the pavement, everything piling up on the grate in front of my house. The water rose even higher in the street.

Scared by the charging water, I sat on the bed in my room. Up here on the third floor, I thought I was safe. But soon I was drawn back to the window, and I realized for the first time that no cars were out on the street. It was too dangerous to drive. If we had to leave the house, how would we get anywhere? My father came in then and told me that the water was spilling over the riverbanks. If the river crested the street curbs we would have go around the corner to the neighbor's house, which had been erected on slightly higher ground.

My father left, and I looked outside again and it was as if the street had never existed. The road had become the river. The sidewalks were now the riverbanks, and the water just got higher and rougher. Ripples and rivulets had become waves and currents in unrelenting rain and mounting winds. The water came pouring from the sky, and ran between the neighbors' houses, under their cars. It grew darker and I knew that the power must have been wiped out because the only light I could see was the hazy moon behind the clouds. Still, I just sat in my room by the window, mesmerized.

I do not remember when I fell asleep that night, but when I woke up the next morning the sun was shining. The cars were still sitting in puddles, but the river had retreated. It amazed me that water could be so dangerous one second, and the next it was all but gone. There was still water on the roofs and in large sidewalk puddles, and there was enough mud for thousands of mud pies, but most of it had drained away overnight.

A week later I asked my father to take me to see the river. By this time the ground was dry again, and all the puddles were gone, but when we walked on the path behind the neighbors' houses I could hear it roaring. By the time we were close enough to see it, the noise was so loud I could hardly hear myself think. The river was a beast, untamable. I thought back to the street water, twisting and churning, transforming the pavement beneath it. This beast in front of me—water surging downstream and carving up the earth—was the last reminder of the storm, and it thrilled me.

ALEXANDRIA COLLINS is a junior at Mt. Ararat High School and she lives in Topsham, Maine. Her story, "When Rain and River Meet," is based on a vivid childhood memory in Lawrence, Massachusetts. She enjoys writing, but her true passion is the performing arts. She is frequently found in the chorus room practicing lines, songs, and dance moves with her friends. One day she hopes to write and direct her own show.

» TIDE POOLS UNDER HOOVES

Hailey Namer

Most people like to visit Popham Beach in Phippsburg, Maine in the summer, to swim and wonder, but I really like it in the winter, because then I can ride horses. After a long drive, my horse, Belle, and I reach the beach. I bring her out of the trailer and she looks overwhelmed. I can tell by the look in her eye. Her pupils are large and her ears perk up. She is alert.

I start by brushing her and tacking her up, putting equipment on. Then I put the lunge rope on and walk down to the beach. There are small waves in the tide pools from other horses' hooves. The sun is fading and the waves are getting smaller. There is at least mist, maybe something more, in the future. After a few minutes of trying, I decide that lunging is not going to work. I hop on her and we start walking.

She does not like the waves. I wonder if she can hear them. She is wearing sponge earplugs. I also wonder if she doesn't like the changing texture of the sand or the tidal pools because her hoof was cut the day before and it could be bothering her. Sand in the cut or salt from the pools would make it sting.

Then, we both start to breathe. I hear her exhale. I

know this is good because it means she is calming down. So we walk the whole beach. I am very happy with her because it is the first time she has been to the beach since I have had her. I really like that the winter beach is pretty much only for a few surfers and people with horses. Winter riding at the beach is my chance to let it all go.

HAILEY NAMER, a sixth grader at Harpswell Coastal Academy, wrote "Tide Pools Under Hooves" when The Telling Room visited her school for three weeks in December. Her story is based on a true experience at Popham Beach in Phippsburg, Maine. She is a competitive horseback rider.

» TEA TIME

Caitlin Conley

When the world is grey
I make a cup of tea.
When the sky falls
And knocks on the door,
Taps on the windows and
Asks to come inside,
It's time for a bold, black tea.
Hot, hot water.
Honey, sugar, cream.
It feels like home.

I watch the steam curl in the air and remember
Blanket-wrapped evenings,
safe and warm. I remember
When my hands were small
And spread wide around a mug.
Laughter of family and friends takes me
To a time when
Everything was perfect.

When the world falls apart
And nothing seems to fit

I sit frozen, clenching fists to temples.
Every muscle tenses,
Each surface is razor sharp,
And every embrace leaves tiny cuts
On my arms, hands, face.
My heart pounds hard against my ribs
Begging to find its way out,
And I know it's time for tea.

CAITLIN CONLEY, a senior at Casco Bay High School, wrote "Tea Time" as a tribute to the many happy memories and comfort she draws from the feeling of a warm, steaming mug of tea. Whether curled up with a good book or camping in the mountains, a cup of tea makes her feel right at home. Caitlin enjoys writing about nature and hopes to pursue a career in outdoor education, combining her passion for the outdoors with her love of the arts.

>> BEHIND THE HELM

Rylie Wareham

At the head of my family's table, there is an empty seat. Five people sit there, while the sixth is out at sea. My mother is making a chicken risotto for dinner and she has set a place for the sixth person. "Oops," she says, "my mistake." The place setting is complete with a fork, a knife, a plate with steaming hot food, and a beer stein with icy water in it. My siblings all laugh at my mother. But when my youngest sibling asks, "Where's Daddy, Mommy?" my mother answers her, and her solemn face devastates us all. For the millionth time, we wonder at our mother's strength, and are grateful for her distractions as she begins for us another story that helps us understand, "Your father..."

When I was just three years old, my mother told me that my life would change. She said that my father would not be around for a lot of my life. I remember crying oceans. The first couple of weeks were hard, definitely, but I would come to realize that that my mother was a strong woman who could pull her own weight with young children, and my father was an important man.

If you think about it, fathers are usually very handy. My father is a Chief Mate who works for Military Sealift Command. He works on a ship for two to six months at a time, and comes home for one-and-a-half to two months before heading out once more. He goes everywhere around the world supplying the Navy, refueling ships, training new Navy Seals, and he also earns a living to keep his family safe, healthy, and happy. When he comes home, we always get so excited and go out for dinner at our favorite restaurant. If my father doesn't come home the day he's supposed to, we don't get too worried. By now, we know that he'll be home soon; it's not because he doesn't love us, it's just because of his job that he's not going to be home on time.

The summer of 2013, my family went to Everett, Washington, to board my father's ship for passage to San Francisco, California. We had been invited by the captain and my father to ride along with them and a bunch of other crewmembers and their families. The ride took four days, and three nights. The ride was smooth, and during the trip, I finally got to see what my father does on a daily basis on his ship. It is pretty amazing. He can instruct a whole crew of men. He organizes everyone at 8 a.m., noon, and at 3 p.m. He tells them what to do for the day, and he also updates everyone on the most recent news.

On the journey, I learned that my father is a highly respected man with many talents. He won Mariner of the Year awards in 2004 and 2007, and is going for his Captain's license soon, which is a long process in which he has to read massive books rich with information about being a captain. He has to learn volumes about ships, marine law, and the laws of nature of the sea, too. It takes a lot of time and effort to become a captain. He explained to us that if he gets his license he would be in charge of a ship, and the weight of the crew and the officers would be on his shoulders. But I know he weighs us as his responsibility, too.

Knowing that my father plays a big part in his job on the sea makes him very prestigious in our family, and we show him lots of respect. He respects us in turn. Though we miss him when he's gone, when my father is sailing out on the ocean we know that he has a well-rounded head on his shoulders, and he has everything under control. And anytime he is home, he has a place at our table. My mother will see to that!

RYLIE WAREHAM, a freshman at Gorham High School, wrote this piece as a graded assignment for her English teacher and as an entry in The Telling Room's annual writing contest. She didn't win the contest, but her story got accepted into the anthology. In her free time, Rylie plays lacrosse, and enjoys field hockey. She also likes football and spending time with her family and friends.

» WE CAN ALL JUMP IN PUDDLES

Elahe Seddiqi

Two years ago, my mother decided that she had to leave Iran so that her five daughters could be educated. My father didn't believe in education for girls, so he wasn't interested in coming with us. He always wanted to have sons instead of daughters. My mom decided to leave her parents and her brothers because of us. It took two years for her to get the permission to immigrate to the U.S. We were told that first we had to go to Slovakia to learn English, fill out the right documents, and get to know the U.S. better.

When we were having meetings about our trip to Slovakia and the United States, the first thing I asked was if we would have to wear headscarves. Everyone laughed at me, but I was relieved when I was told I wouldn't have to wear a scarf. I had given all my girly dresses away. Although I look like a boy, I am really a girl.

In the refugee camp I was called Elahe, a girl's name, but I was mostly a boy to the other boys, and some of the boys were afraid of me because when we fought I beat them up. At the camp, we played every day, too, in the yard with all the other kids. It rains a lot in Slovakia, and one rainy evening my sister Hayde was excited because she

liked it when it rained. Hayde called my sisters Nila and
Mahnaz, some of our friends, and me to play in the rain.
The rain made lots of big puddles. We took our shoes off
and we played tag. We jumped into the puddles barefoot.
We were all muddy and wet but we were having so much
fun. I think happiness is important in life. Happiness is to
laugh and have fun. You can be who you are when you are
happy.

When we came to the United States, my sisters had
more freedom, and I started to think that I could be more
myself, which is a girl. Being a girl means everything: look
at how strong my mom is. I gave away my boy clothes,
like some button-down shirts, and started acting more
comfortable with who I was. When I was in Iran and
Slovakia, being a boy was more fun because parents didn't
worry about boys being outside late at night. If there was
something dangerous, like a tall sliding hill, people didn't
worry about boys going down it. But really, the difference
between a boy and a girl doesn't mean much to me
anymore—we can all jump in puddles. I have experienced
being a boy and being a girl, and I prefer to be myself
because that's who I am, and I love who I am.

*ELAHE SEDDIQI is a sixteen-year-old girl from Afghanistan. She
is a student at Portland High School, and a tenth grader. In her spare
time she paints, walks, watches movies, dances, and writes. She wants the
reader to realize that there is no difference from person to person.*

» EDELWEISS: PORTRAIT OF A GREAT GRANDFATHER

Lizzy Lemieux

He takes me on his knee, the one that's meat and not wood,
Clenching a bone-dry cigar between bony teeth.
All of him needs watering, folded skin like paper cranes,
But he only drinks stronger stuff. And,
He is scared of swimming things, I think.
I look up, head tilted like I'm drinking from his glass,
finding black spaces in his teeth as sharps on a piano,
and every time his lips part to say my nickname, "Edelweiss,"
I try to plunk out melodies I learned this week
in kindergarten. We sink toy boats in the sandbox there,
But the teacher makes them resurface after break.
Maybe she was the one who made him resurface too.
I'm only on the "C" in London Bridge
when he laughs at me.
"Are my teeth too yellow for you, Edelweiss?"
His voice is loud. Small men talk big. He says that.
I shrug, continue banging out the piece,
B, C, D… Which is the part that goes "falling down"
and all I can think of is him falling down,
on the crest of the alps, watering Edelweiss,

which he has such a fondness for,
with his wounds.

LIZZY LEMIEUX, a sophomore at Gorham High School, wrote the poems "Edelweiss: Portrait of a Great-Grandfather" and "The Presumpscot Baptism of a Jewish Girl" as part of her forthcoming collection of poetry, which will be published as part of The Telling Room's Young Emerging Authors Fellowship and is focused on themes of identity and familial history. Her work will appear in Interlochen Arts Academy's journal The Red Wheelbarrow, *the Scholastic Arts & Writing Awards' anthology* Maine Teen Writing of 2015, *and the May 2015 issue of* Maine Magazine. *Next year she will attend Interlochen Arts Academy as the winner of the Virginia B. Ball Creative Writing Scholarship Contest.*

» TORRENTS OF LIQUID

Joseph Ciembroniewicz

The government had shut down the towns surrounding Merrymeeting Bay. Concrete walls topped with barbed wire and gun turrets surrounded the rivers and every other acid well in a hundred-mile radius. Anyone who tried to breach the walls that surrounded the acid sources was shot to death, the body processed into food. Armored trucks trundled through the roads. They however, were not purely militarized. Along with the racks of machine guns and rifles, vats, vials, and rubber tubing lined the berths of the steam wagons.

They had been shut down this way for as long as most could remember, hidden and isolated from the public. Alek Steel spied, from his position in a tree, a strange device on the road that was composed of natural fibers and supposedly fed from a chemical in the air. He jumped down from his lofty perch and started striding through an area densely covered in trees.

Alek glanced at the darkening acid formations in the sky. He knew it was some kind of acid shower, and knew he must find shelter—fast. He strode through the forest of trees, and heard a thunder clap. And then it came. Torrents of liquid, pouring down on him, and he survived. In shock, he strode through the raucous storm and began to forge his way toward a sanction of knowledge where he could seek asylum from the awe that berated him.

The library had been relocated twice: atop a hill in a small storage building that the government now occupied, and now in the deep underground hideaway toward which Alek walked. The entrance was that of an old mine: boarded up around the edges, loose, tetanus-inducing chains hung in front from piercing hooks. The strange library was not advertised or glorified among the locals; most didn't know it existed. Very few approved of reading. Alek thought differently.

As he stepped in, everything changed. The shabby and dilapidated mineshaft that the excuse for a door suggested was a red herring. Alek had learned it was a mythical expression of times past. Instead of gritty, dry, dirt, the floor was covered in fashionable polished coal tiles. Braziers lined the limestone walls, illuminating the overstuffed archives that contained caches of information. Information, and literature. Legendary authors, from hundreds of years ago: Rick Riordan, Gary Paulsen, and his favorite, Philip Reeve. However, he was not there to read about the adventures of Fever Crumb, or Percy Jackson. He wanted information.

A clattering noise echoed throughout the library's central chamber. Looking up from the sagging shelf, Alek winced. A huge blunderbuss was aimed squarely at his face. It was, unmistakably, Berty, the librarian.

Looking a bit disappointed Berty lowered the old gun. "Ah, it's you, Alek. I thought it was one of those government brutes. The nerve of them! Invading our town!" Berty usually had an excuse for pulling out one of his numerous old firearms, despite the fact that his life's ambition was to write a novel. He was ninety-seven years old, towed a typewriter with him everywhere, usually carried more than ten pounds of paper, and was in a torpedo launching wheelchair he had built himself.

"Listen, Berty. I need information on the chemical mixture 'H2O.' I have a...sort of global conspiracy theory."

Without asking questions, Berty brought Alek the one book on H2O he had. It was a thick, leather-bound volume that was cracked and mottled with age. Elegant golden letters formed the words: H2O of the Ages. "That should keep you busy for a while, all that wonderful text about water an—"

The old man could not finish his sentence. There came the clanking of jackboots on the polished floor—the sound of the republic. "Go! They are coming. There's an old minecart further into the library. Take that. I'll hold them off."

"You're nearly one hundred! They'll slaughter you!"

The librarian remained calm. He drew a group of spheres from a pouch on his chair. He picked a machine gun from the wall beside him, and placed an ancient pith helmet on his head. "Maybe they will. I, however, will die defending what I have defended my entire life. Goodbye, Alek. I doubt we will meet again." Berty shoved H2O of the Ages into Alek's hands.

Alek considered it for a few seconds. "Berty, I realized something. The H2O is not poisonous. This entire country is built on lies. I mean to reveal it to the public. Consider that they mistreat us already, forcing us to work as slaves if we are disobedient. They imprison us even with the slightest infraction. I mean to raise a revolution.

I repeat: the H2O is not poisonous." Without waiting for a response, he turned, walking deeper into the maze of shelves and rocky crags.

Berty observed the boy for a moment, and then returned to the problem at hand. He picked up one of the cylinders, and put it into a sort of spring-operated catapult that folded out of his wheelchair arm. He waited for the government thugs to make an appearance from around the corner, and he moved his finger toward a red button, along with the other gadgets of his chair. And he thought. Thought of how the government had murdered his family, how they had forced him into hiding, retired under the earth, waiting for the occasional passerby to turn down the shaft and find his library. It was the government who had brought him to this. Only them. And just like that, the smoldering coals in the old man's heart grew into an inferno of revenge.

The government grunts rounded the corner, and looked a bit dumbfounded when they saw an old disabled man in the hallway with a look of determination plastered onto his face. One spoke, in a rather exasperated voice, "Listen, old man. I don't want to hurt you, but there is something we need at the end of this tunnel. Something that is imperative to our survival. Move aside."

Berty didn't listen. He was in a state of fury. His finger pushed the circular, red, rubber button. There was a click of engaging machinery, and the cylinder flew through the air. It hit the ground. The casing split open. Spikes went flying through the air in all directions. As the invaders fell, darts lodged in their vitals. Berty sighed with relief, glad that in his hasty decision he had chosen a twenty-foot-range flechette grenade, rather than a fifty. He glanced at the core of the missile and its quivering springs, slowly coming to rest.

Returning to reality, Berty realized he was now a killer, and he would be prosecuted without mercy. He turned his chair around, and started rolling toward the minecart track. He did not want to be a murderer. In the moment, Berty had been concerned about the morality of launching his spike-spewing grenade at the invaders. Were five men's lives worth twenty score of books?

He reached the mine track. Aiming carefully, He started trundling down the cart track with the wheels he had designed specially for moving on train tracks in case he needed to escape. The deeper he went, the more hellish the tunnel got. It was dry, hot, and skeletons lined the floor, probably from the numerous mining accidents that had shut the mine down. The old bedrock and digging gear smelled of musty, mouse-eaten books. The light of the first gas lamp had begun to die, and he lit the last one.

The chair picked up speed, and Berty pulled down on the lever that controlled the friction. He checked the valve that told him how much $H2O$ his tank held (the disabled in wheelchairs were given an extra shipment of $H2O$ each day). It was half empty, not a good sign.

At a sudden turn in the tunnel, he saw a minecart in the middle of the track. He shifted the friction control to full, and the chair buckled, stopping mere inches from imminent doom.

"Alek?"

There was no answer. A tray unfolded from the arm of his chair. Without moving his gaze, he opened the wooden box that was on the tray. He slipped the ten rings inside the box onto his fingers. They sprung into strange mechanisms that began to creep up his arms. Two spindly, five-pronged claws sprung from the headrest and unfolded above the cart. Flexing his arms, he moved them forward. The claws followed suit. Then he grabbed at the air in front of him. His fingers felt resistance, and he began to lift.

On the way down, Alek had been terrified. The cart had picked up speed rapidly, and soon was going down the quickly inclining track, at a rate that could prove fatal. Unlike Berty's wheelchair, the cart had no friction control. The track had gone over seemingly bottomless pits, with turns that, if he had been traveling even slightly faster, would have hurled him to his death. At one of these bridges, the cart took an impossibly sharp turn and came to an abrupt dead end. It seemed like an illusion, and in those few milliseconds, he thought it was.

His left leg was extended in front of him. As the cart hit the pile of rocks blockading the track, the leg shattered, bones splintering and ricocheting out like bloody shrapnel. The skin collapsed, leaving his body in a splayed position. His head flew back, crunching against the rusted metal edge of the minecart. His clothing moistened, and began to turn crimson.

The claws lifted the half-dead body, quivering meticulously, probing Alek's oozing leg. Then came the sound of a blade being unsheathed, and in the place of the claw's finger was a huge medical knife. There was a slash, and then the claws began to spew white-hot flames and charred the bloodied stump to stop blood loss.

Moving Alek into a large chamber that most thought contained the motor that piloted him, Berty chuckled to himself slightly, thinking about how he had tricked everyone into thinking he was chair-ridden. Berty stood and began to navigate through the rocks that blocked the track and entered into a place where he least expected to come out. He entered an aqueduct. H_2O sloshed around the stone walk that he stood on. He thought: There will be much to reveal, and a revolt to start.

JOSEPH CIEMBRONIEWICZ lives in Bowdoinham, Maine, and attends Harpswell Coastal Academy. He enjoys writing, but this is his first published story. It is based in a dystopian world where water is hidden from the public. He is twelve years old, plays the violin, enjoys playing "Magic: The Gathering," is devoted to steampunk, listens to John Williams music, and always wears a beret that his headmaster thinks makes him look like Che.

≫ WEB-SLINGING TURTLE

Nina Sprague

My name is Nina. I am a scientist at the Casco Bay Research Institute and I'm going on a lobster boat to do some research for top-secret Experiment #1302.

The boat rocks on the cool blue water like a baby's cradle. Mist drifts over us like a blanket. The ocean waves crashing on the sand are like the sweet hum of a baby's lullaby, and the tree's branches wisp around as if telling their darkest secrets.

As we start heading back, the water seems to turn dark black as if giving a warning. Suddenly the ship stops! I think the ship's motor has given out, but overboard is a turtle holding the ship still with a web-like substance. The crew catches the creature in a net and drags it up carefully before we speed back to my lab on the ship.

I decide to collect data on the turtle so I plan to study the turtle's skeletal system and organs. As I start on the bones near the mouth I see a hole! The turtle is spitting a web out of its mouth. I grab it before the creature can touch it again. The boat arrives at the shore. I thank the captain as I walk up the short dirt road to the Casco Bay Research Institute.

My professor looks at the web under a microscope

and says the only reason it has never been seen before is because the web is like a sphere of invisibility. When the turtle touches it, the turtle automatically becomes invisible. We note that it is also a wonderful net to catch sea cucumbers to eat so that population doesn't grow too high. But there's a problem. The turtles die quickly because they lose blood every time they become invisible.

We have a meeting to decide the turtle's fate. Many scientists want to let it go, but that is impossible since the turtle would think everything was a danger and die in two days. I have an idea and the perfect name for the turtle, too. It wins: 49-33 votes. The turtle is sent to the Marine Animal Aquarium where it lives in a large saltwater tank near a plaque that reads:

"The Web-Slinging Turtle"
Discovered in 2025
By Nina Sprague

NINA SPRAGUE is eleven years old and a fifth grader at Nickerson School in Swanville, Maine. Nina wrote her story in connection with a school trip to the Gulf of Maine Research Institute and a Telling Room prompt. Part of her inspiration came from reading the book Young Man and the Sea *by Rodman Philbrick and a debate in class that was based on an event in the book. When writing this piece, Nina experimented with poetic language and humor in an imaginary, science-related story. When not working hard in school, Nina likes to read, write, act, and play softball.*

» THE SHOWER DRAIN

Jolie Gagnon

The downstairs shower is beautiful, with new soap, the best shampoo, rich conditioner, and a shiny showerhead that sprays an even circle of warm water.

But then there's the drain.

My brother and I won't touch the drain. It growls as hot water slips down it. Its walls are as black and ugly as the tar in our driveway. If someone offered me a billion dollars to walk on the drain, I might, but until then, I will never set foot on it.

"It's easy to clog," my brother says, and I'm pretty sure that's a bad thing. My brother openly says he hates the drain as much as I do. One time when he was little, it ate one of his favorite toys. Now he puts a cloth over the drain to stop the water from going through it.

I remember the day we got our new shower. I was so excited not to share a shower with two guys anymore, my dad and my brother, so I went over to look at it. It was shiny and beautiful. It was too new—it didn't match anything else in our house. I closed my eyes to imagine it later on. I gave it slight mineral stains, the white walls tinted orange, the drain with small bits of rust. Would the drain decay, and maybe even give way under my weight of eighty pounds? I opened my eyes and looked down at the drain. It was shiny and clean…and innocent. Too innocent.

I've read somewhere that shower-related injuries are on the rise. I wonder how many of them are caused by the drain. Probably not many, but we don't know that. Maybe the victims slipped on their drain, not on a stray bar of soap. Could our drains be more evil than we think?

My drain looks evil. It glints and shines with over-inflated pride, as if it enjoys sucking water down to a final resting place. Even though our shower drain looks shiny and innocent, its sharp, cheese-grater holes wait to slice our feet to shreds. If our drains suck down water, could they mutate and suck us down as well?

If our drains really are evil, what can we do? We will need to invent another way to get water out of our showers. We could evaporate the water using hot floors, but then we could burn our feet on the hot floors as well. Or, we could freeze the water into a solid block, but then I suppose we could accidentally freeze our legs in it as well.

Just like monsters under the bed, evil drains are a myth for small kids. When you're young, the world seems out to get you and a simple drain becomes a portal to another world, similar to the closet between Earth and Narnia. A small, regular thing that no one would suspect becomes evil. Are evil shower drains just a myth, a trap for the mind, a story for the people who need to believe? Kids believe in myths and stories, such as sharks in the pool, or an invisible man under the bed. So maybe evil shower drains are just a myth?

But I don't think so. I'm a shy seventh-grade girl here to tell you the shocking reality about shower drains: they are all evil, and they're waiting to drag us into a watery netherworld. Look out below.

JOLIE GAGNON is in the seventh grade at Mt. Ararat Middle School. She lives in Harpswell, Maine, and loves the beach more than anything. Jolie wrote about her shower drain because she loves taking showers, and wanted to try thinking from the drain's point of view. Jolie also plays flute in the Mt. Ararat band, and wants to continue playing in high school. She loved writing with The Telling Room, and hopes to do it again.

>> MY BATHING SUIT SMELLS LIKE MEDICINE

Yann Tanguy Irambona

Some people I swim with on the Deering High School swimming team are in a clique. They don't want a black person on their team. They don't want to make friends. I remember the moment when I was at the team dinner at someone's house and my Burundian friends and I were excluded from the circle. They don't care if we exist, and make me feel that I do not belong here.

The only person I'm close to is my coach. He is the only one who talks to me. After practice my coach tells me if I did well or if I need to practice more. Then one day my coach told me how Portland, Maine, was many years ago—how people had come from other countries to live in the U.S., just like we do today.

My coach told me, "We are all strangers."

I responded, "Yeah, the people from this country, their great-grandparents might be from another country."

Then the coach asked me, "Yann, how did you learn to swim?"

I said, "I learned when I was a kid. I swam for fun not for practice."

The pool here smells like medicine, even my swimsuit does. Thank God I take a shower after practice. Back in my country, the pool smells like palm trees, grass, hot sun, and popcorn from the beach restaurants. Burundi.

Burundi is the great place I used to live in. When I was three years old, I used to go to the pool called Entente Sportive. I was put in a small pool and I was scared. My mom held me and took me into the big pool with her to teach me. Then when I was six years old and I had started to get taller, I went to the medium pool for a couple of months. Finally, I was in the big pool.

That pool was fun. On Saturdays, my dad would wake me up in the morning and say, "Come on, get up and go to swim!" I would reply, "Yeah! I'm ready!" I was always excited when it was Saturday and I got to the pool and saw the sun shining in it. People were happy and I heard a lot of happy voices. Some people were buying food, and others were playing games and jumping in the pool. Smelling the fresh air, always eighty-six degrees, I would hear my friends tell me to come play with them. I felt like I was home with my friends at the pool.

There, you could make new friends you just met at the pool, but back here at the YMCA children practice, they don't play games. In the pool in Burundi children are having fun and there are no lanes, like there are in the YMCA, which separate you.

I remember one day in my country I saw a white Belgian swimming by himself. All of the people were looking at him. My friends told me go talk to him. I said, "No...how about you guys go?" They wouldn't go to talk to him because they were nervous, but I wasn't. I said, "Whatever, I'm going to talk to him." I was nervous but I swam straight to him, shook his hand, and then we talked and we were friends. Now when I remember this, I feel what it felt like to be the stranger in the swimming pool.

I have become the Belgian man on the Deering swim team. I want to tell that the lines in the pool can make you isolated. What I wish is for someone from my swim team and other people from the YMCA to come and cross all the lines to talk to me and say, "Hello," like I did with the Belgian man.

I want the people from my team to have courage to come talk to me and other strangers. But I don't care about those clique people. I swim everyday no longer to look for friends, but to look to my future goals. I think that colleges will like me because I improve every year. I imagine that in five years I'll be a good swimmer in college. I wish that the pool in college could be divided so that half of it has lanes and half is without lanes, because after practice my teammates and I could play games.

YANN TANGUY IRAMBONA is a sophomore at Deering High School, where he is on the swim team and plays baseball. He likes reading, writing, and poetry. He is sure you liked his story—please share it!

⟫ COURAGE IN MILL COVE

Yvette Grady

The ocean has always been my safe place. The rocky slopes, salty smell, and mud flats covered in sea grass have always calmed me. It's been my refuge from the storm inside me. It's the one thing I can always rely on to be there, to never to leave me. Like I had once left myself.

Threading a few fingers through my long, brown hair highlighted by the sun, I gazed across the field at the ribbon of twilight blue ocean gathering in Mill Cove. The reds, oranges, and pinks of the sunset were beginning to fade, leaving the sky a faint pink. I have always loved the view from here. It's my favorite place on Neils Point Road. The road comes between two fields, and there you get a perfect view of the cove on one side and a perfect view of the barn, hay bales, gardens, and the woods behind it on the other. But today I just wanted to see the cove.

I lowered myself to the edge of the pavement and wrapped my arms around my knees as a tear trailed down my cheek and landed on my knee. I have always tried to think of myself as a strong person, but that was the last thing I had been lately.

Seven months ago I was a completely different person. "Happy," "carefree," and "a dreamer" were probably the best words used to describe me. But then, without me knowing it, that all changed. I had thought I was doing the right thing by saying yes. But when I said yes to him, I had no idea how I would end up. No idea it would wreck me.

Another tear fell as I stared at the cove, lost in thought. It had started when I thought I loved him, but I didn't see the reality until it hit me in the face. The reality was that even though I thought I loved him and wanted to stay with him forever, it wasn't going to happen. And we were thirteen. He would be okay. I had to move on and do what it would take to find myself again.

A group of seagulls soared above the cove silhouetted against the pink sky. I watched them wishing I could be up there with them. Wishing I could be away from this. I felt like a piece of me was missing, the part that allowed me to love myself for who I am. The part that was my true personality. The part that knew if he were right for me, then he wouldn't have shot down my dreams with a single word. "I just want myself back," I said softly.

I remember before any of this happened, I loved just lying on my back, staring at the sky, imagining all of the places I wanted to go someday. All the things I wanted to do. How I used to draw, and dream endlessly about finally seeing what was on the other side of the horizon. I remember in March after school every day, I would walk down to the dock, find a wishing rock, and throw it from the end of the pier at the fading pink at the edge of the sky. I missed that.

Looking at the slowly increasing ribbon in the cove, I realized that I could find the person I was. I could take that person and my dreams back. I could be back at the place

I was last March. All it would take was courage. Courage to believe I could be strong and trust that time would heal the cuts I got along the way. I could start painting and dreaming again. Lose myself in the colors and the white noise of the wind at the dock. I would make it out of this storm and be able to look someone in the eyes and say, "I'm okay," and mean it. Nobody could help me. I had to help myself.

I looked out at the almost full cove, and saw a full moon rising over the water and the place where the twilight water was slowly coming in from Casco Bay. I unwrapped my arms from around my legs and wiped tears off my cheeks. I pressed my hands on the pavement, pushing myself up. I stood and gazed at the moon hovering above the water, and took a deep breath. I looked at the water one last time before I turned and began walking toward the barn to check on the ducks on my way home.

I'll make it.

YVETTE GRADY is fourteen years old and a seventh grader at Harpswell Coastal Academy. She wrote this story based on a relationship that had happened a few months prior and how it left her. She decided to write about that particular event because it was a turning point in her life and what she learned she still carries with her today. She enjoys running, drawing, dancing, and spending time with the people she loves.

» SEA FOAM

Isabella Levine

The boat slices through the waves —
a knife through butter.
Foam spurts up from the side,
as waves crash
against the bottom of the boat.
Seagulls take flight,
the wind buffeting their dull white wings
as they squawk their raucous protests
to the salty breeze.

I stare out the sea-pounded window,
scuff my feet
on the grimy green floor,
and watch the towering city buildings —
like great metal trees, tall and proud,
speckled with effulgent lights —
recede in the distance
as we streak across Casco Bay.

The misty foam
puffs up from soft waves,
bubbling, frothing,

white, like snow.
I scoop up a handful of it.
I open my hand
to let it go—
gritty, wet, and light as a cloud—
back to its bondage,
its freedom,
the ocean.

ISABELLA LEVINE, a seventh grader at King Middle School, wrote the poem "Sea Foam" at her school's writing club as two separate pieces, but The Telling Room helped her splice it together as one. She got her inspiration from her life on Peaks Island, and from walks along beaches. In her free time, she loves to read, draw, take photos and write. Isabella also loves to create interesting story beginnings—not that she ever finishes them.

» A DROP IN THE OCEAN

Milly Mpundu

I remember the tall mountains
and the beauty of Rusizi River,
where all the hippopotamus and birds
surrounded its echoes.
I could feel by heart the wild animals' joy
of being in the present.
The time when people loved each other
and wanted the best for each other.

I am so surprised to see that your people,
the ones who agreed to serve you and take care of you,
are actually the ones who turned on you after all you
have done for them.
You were their motherland,
a place that so many of us called home.
A place where everything was settled and graceful at times.
A place that I thought was going to become more
than what it is just today.

You may say that I changed over the years, but deep down
I am still the same kind and curious person
who I have always been.

You could say that my mind and soul have grown,
but it has gotten to a point
where I feel like I have no identity and belonging.
I am like a drop of water that loses its identity
when it joins the ocean.

MILLY MPUNDU is sixteen years old and a junior at Casco Bay High School. She is originally from Burundi and now lives in Portland, Maine. She was inspired to write this poem by the current government events happening in Burundi. During her free time, she likes to watch world news, especially politics. She also volunteers in her community, writes, takes night walks, and loves spending time with her family and friends.

» DOG DISH

Zoe Pinkham

I sit on the counter, staring down at the bowl. Newly bought and cleaned. Clear, fresh water sits in the dish and I wonder how long it will stay in this condition. Serving as the "watering hole" for the animals in my house, it plays an important role. Just as I have this thought, one of the animals approaches.

He stops just in front of it, leaning down to take a long drink of water. I roll my eyes knowing that once my old black lab finishes his drink, this dish will no longer be clean. While coming up for a breath, he turns around to face me. His dark and droopy eyes stare into mine, and I laugh a little as I notice the drool hanging from his lips. Jumping quickly down from the counter and grabbing a paper towel, I wipe it away just before it falls. He drops his head, almost embarrassed that I have to clean up for him. I glance at the clock, noticing it is time for him to eat. As I stand at the closet and start to scoop his food, his eyes light up. Right now, nothing can stop him from getting this food, not even his old and creaking bones. He throws his head back, wagging his tail.

I remember another time when I knew exactly how he felt. We had dropped him off at the vet's office, and he was going to have surgery later that afternoon. He longed for us to stay and he couldn't hide this emotion. Staring at me with his glossy eyes he planted his large body in front of me to try to make this clear to me. He wanted us to run to him, hug him, and bring him home. But we couldn't.

In this moment, too, he can't hide how he feels. He is overcome. Before I set the food down he glances up at me almost smiling, as if to thank me. I don't always pay attention to these moments—his sudden excitement, and the way his usually dark eyes light up. His bones seem no longer to ache, and his vision seems perfect.

He finishes drinking, as quickly as always, taking no breaths. I turn to walk away and he looks back at me. The old seems to spread through him all of a sudden. He walks slower, his bones creaking, and the brightness in his eyes dim.

ZOE PINKHAM lives in Topsham, Maine, and is in her last year at Mt. Ararat Middle School. She shares a home with her family, including three dogs, one of which is her eleven-year-old black lab Bode, the inspiration for the short story "Dog Dish." During her free time, Zoe enjoys writing short stories and poetry, playing soccer, basketball, hockey, and lacrosse, and volunteering at a local elementary school.

≫ GIRLHOOD

Verónica Recalde

Dear girl,
You are standing at the seashore,
Smelling the salt in the water.
Get used to it.
It will carve your nose upright,
Your lips full and red,
Your eyes clear and wide.
This is girlhood.

The salty liquid will pour into your wounds,
Like the words that define you.
The waves will try to sway you.
Plant your feet on the bottom of the sea,
And never let go.
Swim only when you want to —
Use your arms and legs,
Pump up and down,
Roll side to side.
This is girlhood.

There will be rocks at the bottom
Scraping your feet and hands.

Water will fill your lungs.
The words you try to speak will be inaudible.
Try again, speak louder.
You will get thirsty,
The saltwater will never be enough.
Seek all the clear water you need,
Quench your thirst.
This is girlhood.

The unwavering waves
will try to shape you,
Fish-like, sudden and ungraceful.
Their ancient rhythm will remind you
Of the struggle of others.
Honor them.
Swim at your own pace.
This is girlhood.

You will be a woman.
This is your ocean,
Full of beautiful seaweed and dangerous sharks.
This is not a warning, this is a blueprint.
The water will scream that you do not matter.
That you come second.
But you don't.
Stand up, go above the water, to the surface.
That's where you belong.
This is girlhood.
You will survive it.

VERÓNICA RECALDE, an eighteen-year-old, pseudo-junior at Casco Bay High School started living in Maine in the summer of 2014. Originally from Colombia, Verónica decided to spend her gap year before college in Portland, meeting new people and writing new poetry. "Girlhood" is a coming-of-age piece, inspired by her own experiences growing up in a male-dominated society. This piece intends to empower young girls to rise above expectations and prejudices. Verónica's experiences in Colombia and Maine helped her grow as a person and as an aspiring poet.

≫   A BARREL OF TEARS

Maryse Dushime

Oh, BURUNDI! My beautiful motherland.
How I miss your presence.
How I miss your warmth spent on a sunny and beautiful
Sunday with la famille at Saga Plage.
How I miss Tanganyika,
The most crowded place in the country.
Easy to get lost and difficult to be found.
Sitting in the sand while looking for entertainment.

Mother, who would rarely let us enjoy
your vast brown lake.
Instead you released
Your humongous and horrifying waves
To terrify the countries that surround you.
But it was irresistible not to
Dip one's toes under water,
Because you gave hospitality to the crocodile
Gustave le grand
Whose teeth were enormous and deadly.

I can still remember our favorite spot
Because you saved it for us.

"Bonsoir to you all, if you would please allow me
To offer you some of our most wonderful
and thirst-quenching drinks,"
Would say one of our favorite servers.
How welcoming your servants were on behalf of you.
But how long we waited for the food.

Oh, Bujumbura! How I miss you.
The city people.
You gave birth to so many different types
After the arrival of the Belgians,
Who created enemies
That transformed into multitudes of friends and family.

Happy times and distinguished memories
You have gifted me.
But with these memories
You have left me
With a tremendous hole of anguish.
Reminiscing on what could have been;
Gathering around the fire under the country castle
With old friends splitting beans under the night sky.
Listening closely to traditional stories
told by Sogokuru, my grandfather.
"This will keep us united and shall enrich our culture,"
said Data, my father.
Fear fills up my soul
That I may never go back at all.
A barrel of tears
Is all that remains with me.

MARYSE DUSHIME lives in Portland, Maine, and is a sophomore attending Casco Bay High School. She has grown as a writer since she wrote the short poem "Remembering Most of All" at The Telling Room, part of which is excerpted here. During her spare time she prefers to write poetry that reflects on her childhood passed in Bujumbura, her motherland. "Nothing is more appealing than listening to playlists of Yiruma, Wolfgang Amadeus Mozart, or Adele every day," she says.

» WAKE

Emma Levy

The moment a loon emerges from the egg and takes its first shaky step into the water, it is at home. Born to live their entire lives on the waves, loons will never stray far onto land. Even during nesting season, they choose to build their roosts out of lake mud and old reeds in marshy areas just at the water's edge. A loon will only touch dry ground twice in its life: once as he climbs from the nest to begin his watery journey, and once as he climbs ashore to end it.

This past summer, my brother, Jonah, and I were spending one golden afternoon of countless hundreds by the shores of Toddy Pond. The dying warmth of a hot August day enveloped our skin as we sat, side-by-side, on the slippery pebbles by the dock, dangling our feet in the water. We lingered, chatting amiably and watching the shadows reach their trailing fingers across the water until they had swallowed the cove.

A sudden but quiet splash! just to our left startled us. We looked up, scanning the water. Jonah saw it first. He gasped, clasping his hand on my wrist.

"Where?" I breathed.

"There," he whispered. Slowly, cautiously, he nodded

to a shady spot, mere inches away, at the base of a wild blueberry bush growing out over the water.

I saw nothing at first, but as I looked, the shadows beneath the branches began to materialize, and shapes emerged—first, a soft, gracefully curved body, black with a speckling of white; then, bright red eyes and a sharp glinting beak. I had seen one before, of course, dancing along the surface of the water, flapping and laughing in a glorious tremolo. But to be this close, so close I could reach out and touch the velvet slope of his throat, was something I had only dreamed about.

We sat motionless as he emerged from beneath the bush and paddled closer. We barely dared breathe; what if he noticed us and fled? Yet there was something, some sharp awareness in his scarlet eyes, that made me wonder if he had already noticed our presence, and had decided to continue onward anyway—to continue, in the trust that these two curious creatures, gazing at him with wide eyes and stilled breath, would not hurt him; that they were just as enthralled by his presence as he was by theirs. He came closer. Frozen in that moment, the world gone silent around us, we stared, transfixed.

Then it broke. The sunlight glinted off his sharp black beak in just the wrong way, triggering some base instinct telling him that our proximity was not natural, not safe. I twitched before I could stop myself. He blinked, retreated, and vanished into the lengthening shadows.

That was it. He was gone. Still, we remained frozen in that moment, watching as its remnants crumbled around us and reality, with an almost tangible impact, returned. I shook my head as if to clear it of water, and with a shock realized the sun had already begun its descent over the horizon. Night was falling. It was time to leave.

"Jonah," I ventured at last.

He nodded.

"What was he doing?"

"Coming ashore, I think," Jonah responded.

"Coming ashore? But—" I stopped. We looked at one another. Paused. We both knew, all too well, what "coming ashore" meant for a loon. Yet neither of us seemed quite able, at the moment, to voice it.

As we made our way back to the house, Jonah ahead of me on the path, I turned back to look at the soft sand by the water's edge where we had been sitting just moments before. Perhaps it would be later tonight, when we had long been curled up in our beds with the fans pulling the cool summer air in through the window, and when the shore was once again undisturbed, that he would return. He would nestle himself into the sand just as he had burrowed into his mother's feathers when he was a chick. And the waves would wash over, pulling him from the sand. He would settle at the bottom, his bones to be washed by the soft, teal waters of the lake, rolling in the currents, back where he belonged.

EMMA LEVY, a junior at Mt. Ararat High School in Topsham, wrote "Wake" as an homage to her beloved older brother and the summers they spend together with the loons in their family's camp on the shores of Toddy Pond. During her free time, Emma loves to ski and run, play pop songs on the flute and piano (especially those by Maroon 5), and curl up with a good book and a crafting project.

» BODIES OF WATER

Henry Spritz

They were bodies of water,
in the water, on the water, with the water,
pulled from cottages,
leaving screen doors swinging,
bolting down greens lawns
in a sprint that ended in a crescendo
of foam and splash and spray.

Escaping the heat, the house,
finding refuge
in that moment of weightlessness
when their feet left the pebbly sand
and the ocean seemed to sink back
in anticipation.

In that one moment,
they could see the dark
and the green and the blue all mixed together
like a painter's easel. They could see the dark
rippling movement of guppies
and spot the urchins
and starfish basking

on barnacle-speckled rocks.

They saw all that,
and then felt the cool sea
rushing up their backs
and into their hair,
pulling them
into an embrace.

And after they emerged, they moved
to the sunburnt dock
chalked by dried salt footprints.
They leapt and twirled and flipped
until the sun dove into the ocean as well,
joining them and disappearing from view
under the waves.

Even when the moon sat
frozen over the water,
the sounds of splashing
echoed off the rocks,
and dormant lawn chairs,
and up the green lawns,
and then flowed back
to reverberate across the sea
until the sun shone once more.

HENRY SPRITZ, an eighth grader at King Middle School in Portland, became involved with The Telling Room when he was one of four students in the newly created Young Emerging Authors Fellowship program. An excerpt from The Road to Terrencefield *(2014), the book he wrote with The Telling Room, won a Scholastic Art & Writing Gold Key Award in the State of Maine. His piece, "Bodies of Water," is based on his own summer experiences.*

» ACKNOWLEDGMENTS

A tremendous congratulations to this year's esteemed editors in The Telling Room's Publishing Workshop: student editorial interns Emily Denbow, Joel Kahn, and Verónica Recalde, who were joined by professional writers and editors Molly McGrath, Caitlin Guthiel, Alex Acquisto, and Rose Heithoff. Every Wednesday afternoon for thirteen weeks, the Publishing Workshop gathered on the fifth floor at 225 Commercial Street to create this book.

When the Sea Spoke is the product of hours of reading and rereading, clicking and clacking on keyboards, and scritch-scratching on paper. In a vast ocean of student stories, we found forty brilliant pieces bobbing like buoys and took them ashore. With care we worked with each author to revise and refine, being sure to keep the initial spark and shine that caught our eyes. We became a trusty crew aboard the ship we built ourselves, and *When the Sea Spoke* became both our compass and the destination.

The stories and poems in this book sprung from the following Telling Room programs: Young Writers & Leaders, Young Emerging Authors Fellowship, WordPLAY, In School Residencies with Mt. Ararat Middle School, Harpswell Coastal Academy, and Cultivating Community, The Telling Room Writing Contest, Publishing Workshop, and our partnership with the Gulf of Maine Research Institute.

We would like to thank the incredible teaching staff of these programs: Molly Haley, Sonya Tomlinson, Patty Hagge, Molly McGrath, Andrew Griswold, Laura McCandlish, Katy Kelleher, Marjolaine Whittlesey, Sean Lynch, and Katy Sargent. We would also like to thank the teachers and administrators–Kimberly Emerson at Mt. Ararat Middle School, John D'Anieri and Rory Wall at Harpswell Coastal Academy, Lucinda Stein at Gorham High School, Patty Ferrentino at Nickerson School, and Meredith Cass at Mt. Ararat High School–for their guidance and for the strong encouragement they gave their students. Huge thanks to the many devoted Telling Room volunteers as well for making this work possible.

These programs could not have taken place without the generous support of the Emanuel & Pauline A. Lerner Foundation, Beim Foundation, Edward H. Daveis Benevolent Fund of the Maine Community Foundation, MainStreet Foundation of Androscoggin Bank, Moser Family Foundation, Quimby Family Foundation, Ronald McDonald House Charities of Maine, Jane B. Cook 1992 Charitable Trust, Morton-Kelly Charitable Trust, Margaret E. Burnham Charitable Trust, Sam L. Cohen Foundation, Rines/Thompson Fund of the Maine Community Foundation, Old Bug Light Charitable Foundation, and the Rumphius Foundation. This project was also funded in part by a grant from the Maine Arts Commission, an independent state agency supported by the National Endowment for the Arts.

≫ ABOUT THE TELLING ROOM

The Telling Room is a nonprofit writing center in Portland, Maine, dedicated to the idea that children and young adults are natural storytellers. Focused on young writers ages 6 to 18, we seek to build confidence, strengthen literacy skills, and provide real audiences for our students' stories. We believe that the power of creative expression can change our communities and prepare our youth for future success.

Our fun, innovative programs enlist the support of local writers, artists, teachers, and community groups. At our downtown writing center we offer free afterschool workshops and tutoring, and host field trips for school groups from all over Maine. We also lead workshops at local schools and community organizations; bring acclaimed writers to Maine to give public readings and work with small groups of students; publish bestselling anthologies of student work and books like this one by our young authors; and carry out community-wide storytelling projects and events.

We serve those who are reluctant to write as well as those who already identify as writers, including: children and young adults who are a part of Maine's growing community of immigrants and refugees, those with emotional and behavioral challenges, students struggling in mainstream classrooms, homeschoolers enthusiastic to join a creative community, and passionate young writers who need additional support beyond what their schools are able to provide.

www.tellingroom.org

TELLING ROOM BOOKS

Other titles by The Telling Room:

10th Anniversary Anthology

The Story I Want to Tell

Student Anthologies

Beyond the Picket Fence
Illumination
Exit 13
How to Climb Trees
Can I Call You Cheesecake?
Tearing Down the Playground
I Carry It Everywhere
I Remember Warm Rain

Telling Room Authors

Forced by Zahro Hassan
Sleeping Through Thunder by Grace Roberts
Hemingway's Ghost by Noah Williams
Between Two Rivers by Aruna Kenyi
Fufu and Fresh Strawberries by Caitlin Lowell
and Charlotte McDonald

Find these books at:
tellingroom.org/store
or your local bookseller.

All proceeds from the sale of Telling Room books
support our free writing programs for Maine youth.